St. Louis Community College

Library

5801 Wilson Avenue
St. Louis, Missouri 63110

EDWARD S. CURTIS

Edward S. Curtis (1868–1952)

EDWARD S. CURTIS

Photographer of the North American Indian

Victor Boesen and
Florence Curtis Graybill

Illustrated with photographs

DODD, MEAD & COMPANY · NEW YORK

Photographs courtesy of: page 53, The Pierpont Morgan Library; page 56, the Museum of the American Indian, Heye Foundation; page 116, the British Columbia Provincial Museum, Victoria, British Columbia. All other photographs, courtesy of Jean-Antony du Lac/The Curtis Project.

Library of Congress Cataloging in Publication Data

Boesen, Victor.
    Edward S. Curtis, photographer of the North American
Indian.

    Includes index.
    SUMMARY: A biography of Edward Curtis who
spent many years photographing, writing about, and
recording the songs of the North American Indians.
    1. Curtis, Edward S., 1868–1952—Juvenile litera-
ture. 2. Photographers—United States—Biography—
Juvenile literature. 3. Indians of North America—
Juvenile literature. [1. Curtis, Edward S., 1868–1952.
2. Photographers. 3. Indians of North America] I.
Graybill, Florence Curtis, joint author.
TR140.C82B63   770′.92′4 [B] [92] 76–53435
ISBN 0–396–07430–8

To the Indians of North America

Acknowledgments

We are grateful, first of all, to Librarian Ruth M. Christensen of the Southwest Museum, who brought forward the forty-four-year correspondence between Curtis and editor Hodge. The existence of this correspondence, beginning in 1903 and ending in 1947, had been unknown even to members of Curtis's family. Others who helped us get the story were Renate Hayum, History Department, Seattle Public Library; Andrew F. Johnson, University of Washington Libraries; Beverly Russell, Chief Librarian, Seattle *Times*; the Newspaper Reference Library, Spokane, Washington; Amy E. Levin, Reference Librarian, Smithsonian Institution Libraries, Washington, D.C.; Manford E. Magnuson, Angus McMillan, and James R. Cumming, Cumming Associates, Genealogists.

Authors' Note

The material for the book came from Curtis's memoirs, which he reluctantly undertook late in life at his family's insistence, but never completed; from notes of talks with their father by Florence and Katherine; Curtis's log of his trip to the Far North in 1927, his final field trip; his letters to Harriet Leitch, reference librarian at the Seattle Public Library, a few years before his death; from the correspondence between Curtis and his editor, the noted Indian authority, Frederick Webb Hodge, at the Smithsonian Institution in Washington, D.C., later Director of the Southwest Museum in Los Angeles; and from Curtis's twenty volumes themselves.

More material came from such published sources as existed, including Ralph Andrews' *Curtis' Western Indians,* the work of A. D. Coleman and T. C. McLuhan, and numerous newspaper and magazine articles.

Contents

1. Vanishing Race

Edward Curtis's eyes widened. He spread the newspaper and held it closer. In Rochester, New York, he read, a man named George Eastman had invented a dry plate to take the place of the wet plate in photography. The new plate brought exposure time down to a fraction of a second, the account went on, and it made picture-taking much simpler. Eastman's invention meant that the photographer no longer needed to mix materials and prepare his own plates; he could buy them, ready to use.

Popular interest in photography was already high at the time. It had been growing ever since Professor John William Draper of New York University, in 1840, made a portrait of his daughter, Dorothy Catherine, becoming the first man to capture the human face on a photographic plate. He exposed the plate for six minutes in bright sunlight. In England not long afterward, the well-known portrait artist, David Octavius Hill, put down his brushes and instead used the camera to complete a goal of 400 portraits he had set himself. Among the many who became camera fans was Lewis Carroll, author of *Alice's Adventures in Wonderland*, who took pictures of his friends, including John Ruskin, Alfred Lord Tennyson, and little Alice Pleasance Liddell, the "Alice" of his famous book.

Photography as we know it today was still far in the future, but Eastman's dry plate greatly simplified procedures. Picture-taking became a common pastime, and top artists experimented with the camera as an instrument of self-expression, among them James McNeill Whistler and John Singer Sargent.

As Edward went about his chores on the farm, he dreamed of owning a camera—but the hope was dim. The Curtis family was poor. There was hardly money enough for the basic needs of life.

With the sensitivity of youth, Edward could not forget the day when the presiding elder of the church rode up on his horse at suppertime. Edward's mother called him aside and in a hushed tone said, "What shall we do? We can't just give the elder boiled potatoes. That would be terrible." She thought a moment. "Is that old snapping turtle still down at the creek?"

"Yes," Edward answered, inwardly wincing at the thought in his mother's mind. The turtle was a pet.

"You go and get him and butcher him," she instructed.

When the turtle had been prepared and put on the table, Edward's mother quietly summoned him and the other children—Ray, Asahel, and Eva—to her side. "You children and I will say we're not really hungry," she said. "Leave the meat for your father and the elder."

Each spring and autumn, the Curtis family looked forward to a feast of smoked muskrat legs. These were brought home by Edward's father, the Reverend Johnson Curtis, from his biannual pilgrimage by canoe to call on his parishioners, widely scattered through the Minnesota woods. He took Edward along "for the good of his soul" and to see the country, but also, Edward suspected, to help with the paddling and portaging.

For Edward, though, there were other rewards from these wilderness journeys with his father. He developed a fondness for the free and self-reliant life of the woods—for knowing nature, for cooking over camp-fires, sleeping in the open—all of which would serve him well in the years to come. And it made him want a camera all the more. The out-doors was filled with things to take pictures of.

Like many others, Edward decided to build his own. He borrowed a manual showing him how and set to work. It was a simple task. He fitted a wooden box inside another, made to slide in and out. He fixed

Johnson Curtis, Edward's father

Ellen Sherriff, Edward's mother

a panel of ground glass at the back, and at the front installed a stereopticon lens which his father had brought home from the Civil War. This was not far from all there was to it.

From a copy of *Wilson's Quarter Century In Photography*, "A Collection of Hints on Pictorial Photography which form A Complete Text-Book of the Art," by Edward Livingston Wilson of Philadelphia, Edward received a basic education in the use of the camera.

The book by Wilson, who wrote in his preface that he had taken up photography twenty-five years earlier in the face of warnings that it was "a circus kind of a business, destined to a short life, and unfit for a gentleman to engage in," contained 528 pages and seemingly left little else to be said on the subject. Wilson had made good on his objective, as he wrote, to make the volume "useful alike to learner and earner—a book fully up to the times, and helpful for all time."

To gain experience, Edward worked for a time in a St. Paul photo shop. Then he set up a shop of his own, but the people of the little backwoods community where he lived were as poor as the Curtis family, and the enterprise failed.

Edward's father was in frail health, and Edward needed to earn money to help support the family. He put aside his camera and although he was not yet eighteen—but over six feet tall—he found work as boss of 250 French-Canadians building the Soo Line railroad. "They didn't understand me, and I didn't understand them," Edward remembered, "but we got the job done."

In the autumn of 1887, Edward went with his father to the Territory of Washington, at the far northwest corner of the country, to prepare the way for the rest of the family to follow in the spring. The elder Curtis believed that the milder climate of the Seattle area might help him.

He and Edward found a place to homestead on the labyrinth of waterways that form Puget Sound, near what became Port Orchard. From the thick spruce woods all about, with ax and saw, they cut trees and built a log cabin, Edward doing the heavy work. The new country, where it rained instead of snowed as winter came and no one suffered from the cold, promised the Curtis family a good life.

But for Johnson Curtis life ended in a year, leaving Edward to become the mainstay of the family. Ray, his older brother, had married and gone his own way. Edward spaded gardens, chopped wood, built fences, ran errands—and in spare moments took pictures, so far as is known, with his homemade camera.

Also, he found time for Clara, one of several sisters in the Phillips family, living not far away. Clara was bright and shared his interest in the outdoors. In 1892, at the age of twenty-four, Edward married her. Near the same time, as befitted his new responsibilities, he borrowed $150 and bought a photo studio, which in due course became known as the right place in town to have one's picture taken. The studio especially attracted the daughters of well-to-do families, who believed that having their portraits made by Edward Curtis—who by now wore a Vandyke beard, enhancing his native aristocratic appearance—gave them glamor.

Studio photography lost interest for Edward, however, and gradually he left the routine of the studio to assistants, spending more and more time outside. He became a familiar figure as he wandered about the environs of the city, carrying a big 14 x 17 inch view camera, which he had bought from a prospector on his way to the California goldfields.

One evening he came upon old Princess Angeline, daughter of Chief Seattle, the city's namesake, digging clams near the shanty where she lived on the waterfront. Edward dug into his pocket and held up a silver dollar, at the same time pointing to his camera.

She understood, grinning and nodding approval. "I paid the princess a dollar for each picture I made," Edward recalled years later. "This seemed to please her greatly and she indicated that she preferred to spend her time having pictures taken to digging clams."

The satisfaction was mutual. Edward liked his photographs of Angeline, his very first of an Indian. He visited the Tulalip Reservation and shot pictures of Indians all day, returning a day or two later and taking yet more photographs. He gained the confidence of the Indians by treating them as equals. "I said 'we,' not 'you,' " he explained. "In other words, I worked with them and not at them."

After he had taken pictures of Indians for a couple of years, Edward

Princess Angeline

selected three from his collection, including the one of Princess Angeline, and entered them in a national photographic exhibition. His photographs won the grand prize. The pictures were sent on a tour overseas and won laurels wherever they went. One of the pictures, *Homeward*, showing a party of Indians in a boat silhouetted against the sunset, won a gold medal.

Edward's Indian photographs also added modestly to his income. Sold at his studio and at other outlets in the city, the prints were bought chiefly by visitors to Seattle who wanted to show the folks at home there were still Indians around. In a small studio brochure, he placed the photography of Indians ahead of his other work. "Curtis Indians," the brochure was marked in front. On the back appeared the name of the studio, followed by "Home of the Curtis Indians" and then "Photo Portraiture"—in that order.

Meanwhile, other subjects as well caught Edward's eye. The Puget Sound country was a photographer's paradise. To the west rose the sawtooth range of the Olympic Mountains, their snow-mantled peaks reaching from the Juan de Fuca Strait on the north to the Columbia River on the south. Paralleling the Olympics on the east sat the Cascades, thrusting against the clouds for 200 miles, north to south. So clearly limned were the rugged shapes of these enclosing mountain ranges, that they seemed no more than 5 or 10 miles away, rather than 20 to 80.

As he looked northeast across the verdant, forest-covered basin cradling the many-fingered contours of Puget Sound with its 2,000 miles of shoreline, Edward's eye invariably fell on silver-topped, 11,000-foot Mount Baker; and when he glanced to the southeast, in the direction of Tacoma, he saw Mount Rainier. Covering an area the size of Rhode Island and nearly 3 miles high, Rainier stood alone on the plain, like Japan's sacred Fujiyama. On moonlit nights, the glow of her peak could be seen 40 miles, distinct enough to photograph.

It was no wonder, Edward thought, that the people of Seattle possessively called Rainier "our mountain," while those of Tacoma claimed it as theirs, referring to it as Mount Tacoma.

Drawn to this majestic landmark, Edward became an expert alpinist as he explored the mountain's scenic treasures with his camera, heavy pack of glass plates on his back—the rivers of ice creeping down her sides, the streams, lakes, and waterfalls—forests so dense no breeze stirred the leaves, and the gloom of night lying everywhere.

One evening as he made camp at the 10,000-foot level, at the site marked by naturalist John Muir as the place to get a night's rest before going on to the top next morning, Edward sighted a group of men in the distant twilight, making their way across mile-wide Nisqually

Homeward

Glacier. Watching them for a few moments, Edward sensed that they were tenderfoots, unaware of the crevasses hidden under the snow. A man could vanish into one of these and never be seen again.

Edward hurried off to give warning. "I guess we're lost," one of the strangers admitted. He was shivering and stamping his feet as Edward came up.

"You better come to my camp," Edward suggested, explaining about the crevasses. "Go on in the morning, when you can see where you're going." All agreed that was a good idea.

Edward led the way to safety. As he threw more wood on the fire, the strangers gathered around the warming flames and introduced themselves. All were prominent men from Washington, D.C. One was Dr. C. Hart Merriam, physician and naturalist, who was chief of the United States Biological Survey. A second was Gifford Pinchot, head of the Division of Forestry, later to become governor of Pennsylvania. A third was George Bird Grinnell, editor of *Forest and Stream*, in addition to being a naturalist and authority on Indian life well-known for his books about the Plains Indians.

The group was on a mission to study Mount Rainier, and in Edward they soon realized that they had found a rich source of information. The talk around the campfire went on most of the night. Next morning the visitors asked Edward to be their guide for the rest of their stay on the mountain.

"You would be a great help to us," they said.

Edward accepted. "I'll get some good pictures as we go," he replied. By this accident of fate he began friendships which would mold his future.

During the rest of the winter, having found much in common to discuss on the mountain, Edward and Grinnell kept in touch by mail. In the spring Edward received a letter from Grinnell saying that E. H. Harriman, the railroad magnate, planned a scientific expedition to Alaska, then in the world spotlight for the discovery of gold. At first Harriman had in mind only a holiday cruise with his family to hunt the Kodiak bear, but had been persuaded by the men Edward had met on Mount Rainier to turn the trip into a full-scale scientific voyage.

The Clam Digger

"Mr. Harriman commissioned Mr. Merriam and myself to round up qualified people to go along," Grinnell wrote. "We would like to have you with us as chief photographer."

As the *George W. Elder* weighed anchor at Seattle on May 30, 1899, and set course for the northland, Edward found himself in heady company. It was his first association, he remembered, "with men of letters and millionaires." The passenger list read like a *Who's Who* of American science. Among them were the legendary John Burroughs, who became the nation's best known and best loved naturalist; and Burroughs' friend, the renown John Muir, the Scottish-born nature lover whose efforts led to the founding of Yosemite and other national parks.

Muir wrote afterward that one of the most exciting moments of the whole trip for him came as Edward and his assistant, D. G. Inverarity, were taking pictures from a small canvas canoe under the face of Muir Glacier, discovered by Muir some time before. The boat rode precariously low in the water, and to Muir and the others, nervously watching from a hill, it looked as if at any moment it might be swamped.

All at once a huge chunk broke from the glacier and plunged into the sea, throwing up a mountainous wave. The little boat disappeared, then was tossed high on the crest of a new wave, only to be lost from sight a second time as yet another section of ice thundered into the water. The spectators on the hill turned away, certain they had seen a tragedy. When they looked again, the boat was back in full view, Edward and Inverarity busily taking pictures as if nothing had happened.

The sun came up early and went down late in the Alaska summer, and Edward was pleased by what Harriman said to him at the outset of the voyage: "The summer days are long on both ends, and I urge that you make use of all the daylight we have."

Edward eagerly became one of the hardest working members of the expedition, taking time for little else than his camera. The voyage reached to the shores of Siberia, and during the two months it lasted, Edward and his assistant took more than 5,000 pictures. These included photographs of some 600 plant and animal species new to science, as well as glaciers and other geographic features. Edward's pictures of Indians on the trip established him as a master of this subject.

The expedition gave Edward an opportunity to cement his friendship with George Bird Grinnell, who was known as "Father of the Blackfoot People" for his work with the Blackfoot Indians of Montana, among whom Grinnell had spent the past twenty summers. "Come with me next year," he invited Edward as they stood at the rail of the ship on the way home. "You'll have a chance to know Indians—and find out how they feel about things."

Thus, on an afternoon a few months later, Edward and Grinnell sat astride their horses on a high bluff overlooking the Piegan Reservation in Montana. Flung out before them as far as they could see, the prairie was covered with tipis of Indians gathering for their annual sun dance. To Edward the scene was overwhelming. In Seattle he was used to seeing Indians by ones and twos. Here he was seeing thousands.

"The sight of that great encampment of prairie Indians was unforgettable," he wrote years later. "Neither house nor fence marred the landscape. The broad, undulating prairie stretching toward the Little Rockies, miles to the west, was carpeted with tipis. The Bloods and Blackfeet from Canada were also arriving for a visit with their fellow Algonquins."

There were men and women riding horses, some traveling by wagon; camp equipment, personal effects, babies and pups hauled by travois, the transport device made of two poles held together by a frame and drawn by horse.

For many minutes the two men watched in silence as the spectacle unfolded on the plain below. "Take a good look," Grinnell said at last. "We're not going to see this kind of thing much longer. It already belongs to the past."

Grinnell spoke the words in Edward's mind. More and more the white man was spreading over the plains, laying out farms and ranches and building towns and cities, lacing the whole together with roads and railways that often trespassed across the reservations on which he sought to confine the Indian. Standing by at strategically placed forts, the United States Cavalry was ready to ride the moment the Indian rose in protest against the continuing violation of the treaties which the "Great Father" in Washington kept making with the red man.

The buffalo, chief source of food for the plains Indians, had become a rarity. The animal had been nearly wiped out by the encroaching whites, who systematically slaughtered more than 3 million of the beasts during a two-year killing frenzy in the early seventies, all to starve the Indians and "allow civilization to advance," as it was put by Civil War hero General Phillip Sheridan. Yes, without question, in only a few more years the Indian way of life as Edward and Grinnell now were seeing it from their horses on the bluff, would be gone.

Camp in the Foothills—Piegan

East of the Mississippi River, the Indian as he had been found by the early settlers had long ago vanished. What he was like, what he believed, how he lived—outside the fictional portrayals of James Fenimore Cooper—no one really knew. Unknown, he had gone unknown into oblivion.

As Edward and Grinnell mingled with the Indians during the next couple of weeks—at their campfires, in their tipis, watching as they went through the self-torture of the sun dance—an idea formed in Edward's mind. This was to see that what happened to the eastern Indian did not happen to his western counterpart. With his camera Edward resolved to make a record of these first inhabitants of the country.

As much as possible he would preserve on film what the Indian looked like, the things that were of him and by him, and what he did from day to day. What he was unable to capture with his camera he would tell in descriptive titles to go with the pictures.

Grinnell heartily approved. "Count on me for anything I can do to help," he said. As the author of *Pawnee Hero Stories, Blackfoot Lodge Tales, The Story of the Indian,* and many others, Grinnell knew a great deal about Indians. He guided Edward in the things to look for as he went abroad among them with his camera.

"You realize of course that this is a big undertaking," he cautioned. "There are very many tribes, each one different. Each has its own language, its own customs, its own traditions. Everything is different— what they wear, what they eat, what they believe. It's going to take time—a lot of time; and you'll need money."

"I think I can do it in fifteen years," Edward replied. "I can sell my prints as I go. That should meet my costs."

Chaíwa—*Tewa*

2. Transcriptions for Future Generations

Edward said good-by to Grinnell and hurried home to Seattle. He bought supplies and equipment, and made arrangements at the studio to be away for an extended time. Ten days after he had sat with Grinnell overlooking the Montana plain, he was in southern Arizona, hard at work with his camera among the Hopi Indians.

Edward was not the first to make pictures of Indians. The "red man" had been a popular subject with artists and photographers for nearly seventy-five years. Among the first was George Catlin, who practiced law in Philadelphia for a couple of years, but then took up the study of art and became a portrait painter in New York City. In 1832 Catlin went west to study and paint the Indian, for the most part devoting the rest of his life to this.

The greater part of Catlin's 470 full-length portraits of the Indians and of tribal scenes ended up at the National Museum in Washington, D.C., while his 700 sketches went to the American Museum of Natural History in New York City.

Another who preceded Edward in portraying the Indian was Captain Seth Eastman of the United States Army. In 1850, steel engravings from Eastman's drawings were used to illustrate a six-volume work about Indians by Henry Schoolcraft—explorer, geologist, and student of the Indian.

The first man to use the camera to portray the Indian appears to have been William Henry Jackson, who began well before Edward was born.

Walpi

Traveling in a buggy fitted with a darkroom, Jackson took pictures of all sorts of western subjects—Indians, cowboys, stagecoaches, wagon trains, and of Pony Express riders, the Bible-toting young men who in 1860 carried the mail by horseback between St. Joseph, Missouri, and Sacramento, California—2,000 miles—on a ten-day schedule.

Will Soule took pictures of the Indians around Fort Sill, Oklahoma, while Adam Clark Vroman favored those of the Southwest as subjects—those with whom Edward was now beginning. There were others, more obscure, who photographed the Indian before Edward. "Shadow catchers," the Indians called them.

A Walpi Man

But no one had gone about it as Edward was doing: with an orderly, comprehensive plan, intending to stay with it until he had completed a full-scale photographic record of the American Indian west of the Mississippi, hurrying to get it done while there was still time. The undertaking was as bold as it was novel and heroic.

The Potter

At this point, though, Edward had no idea how big and protracted the project would become—that what he had started in the heat of the southwestern desert would end in a howling gale near the Arctic Circle half a lifetime later; that there would be time for little else through the years—only hard work sixteen hours a day, seven days a week.

"Following the Indian's form of naming man I would be termed The Man Who Never Took Time To Play," Edward reminisced when he was eighty-three.

The Piki Maker

But one thing in these beginning days was very clear in his mind. "I made one resolve, that the pictures should be made according to the best of modern methods and of a size that the face might be studied as the Indian's own flesh," he remembered long afterward. "And above all, none of these pictures would admit anything which betokened civilization, whether in an article of dress or landscapes or objects on the ground.

"These pictures were to be transcriptions for future generations that they might behold the Indian as nearly lifelike as possible as he moved about before he ever saw a paleface or knew there was anything human or in nature other than what he himself had seen."

At the outset, the Indians were cool to Edward. They had no more reason to care for him than for other white men, whose view of the world around them was very different from their own. As it was movingly expressed by Chief Standing Bear of the Poncas, "We do not think of the great open plains, the beautiful rolling hills, and winding streams with tangled growth as wild," he said.

"Only to the white man was nature a wilderness and only to him was the land infested with wild animals and savage people. To us it was tame. Earth was bountiful and we were surrounded with the blessings of the Great Mystery. Not until the hairy men from the east came and with brutal frenzy heaped injustices upon us and the families we loved was it wild for us. When the very animals of the forest began fleeing from his approach, then it was for us that the Wild West began."

Edward was likewise handicapped by his ignorance of the Indian; he knew as little about him as the next paleface. Thus he made the usual mistakes, such as thinking of the Indians' religion as a "superstition," and being too forward. Three or four times he heard the crack of a rifle shot in some unseen quarter, followed by the whine of a bullet past his ear. On several occasions the Indians perversely crowded in front of his lens, keeping him from getting his picture. Once he was charged by a drunken Indian on horseback, grabbing his camera and leaping aside just in time to avoid being trampled.

Another time an Indian scooped up handfuls of dirt and threw

Kachina Dolls

them at the camera—only to be startled as Edward this time stood his ground, drawing his knife and rushing the offender.

Edward was learning. By showing he was no coward, both the offender and the other Indians, who applauded Edward's action, saw him in a new light—as someone to respect.

Edward showed the Indians that once they had made an agreement with him, he expected them to keep it, gaining further stature in their eyes. Once, as he photographed among the Zuñis, paying them fifty cents each to pose—half a day's working wage in those times—they stopped showing up after a day or two. The chief cannily explained

the problem to Edward. "I have told them it is bad luck to pose for fifty cents," he said.

Edward indicated, on the contrary, that it would be bad luck if they did not. "I will stay in the village two more days," he said coolly, taking down his tripod. "If they are not back by then, they will lose their chance."

There was no more problem.

Edward found it useful, likewise, to discover as time passed that the Indian looked upon the white man as his inferior. This alerted him that he began with a disadvantage, which he could hope to overcome. He learned to be himself around the Indians, rather than imitate them. He wore his own clothes. He made friends with their children and with their dogs, just as he would do in the white man's community.

But perhaps the most important thing that won him approval from the Indians as he worked among them was that in his heart he liked them. They sensed this. "An Indian is like an animal or small child," he once said. "They instinctively know whether you like them, or if you're patronizing them. They knew I liked them and was trying to do something for them."

In the end, Edward was accepted by the Indians as more than a friend, but as one of their own. "He is just like us," they would say as Edward sat with them in their tipis, all smoking and chatting with the easy familiarity of old intimates. "He know about the Great Mystery."

In 1911, when the project had grown to include text as well as pictures, Edward explained to a *New York Times* reporter how he got the Indians to cooperate. "Many of them are not only willing but anxious to help. They have grasped the idea that this is to be a permanent memorial of their race, and it appeals to their imagination. Word passes from tribe to tribe. . . . A tribe that I have visited and studied lets another tribe know that after the present generation has passed away men will know from this record what they were like, and what they did, and the second tribe doesn't want to be left out."

Edward went on to tell how tribes still four or five years away on his schedule would send word asking him to come and see them. "Where they haven't hit upon the idea themselves I suggest it to them," Edward said. "I say, 'Such and such a tribe will be in this record and you won't. Your children will try to find you in it and won't be able, and they will think you didn't amount to anything at all, while the other tribe will be thought to be big people.'"

For a while even this approach didn't work with Chief Black Eagle, a leather-faced patriarch of the Assiniboin tribe. In all his ninety years Black Eagle had stubbornly refused to tell the white man a thing, either of himself or his people, and he clearly had no intention of starting with Edward. All day the old chief maintained a haughty silence, refusing even to allow his picture to be taken.

In the small hours of next morning, Edward was shaken awake by a

A Painted Tipi—Assiniboin

Assiniboin Hunter

hand on his shoulder as he lay sleeping in his tent. Fumblingly lighting his lantern, he made out Black Eagle standing beside his cot. For a confused moment, remembering the chief's attitude toward him during the day, Edward thought he might be in for a lot worse trouble.

"I have been told you are writing a book about Indians," Black Eagle rumbled in the half-light, as if he hadn't known what Edward was doing.

"That's right," Edward answered, gathering his wits.

"Will there be something in it about Black Eagle?"

"There will if you'll tell me something to write," Edward retorted, by now fully awake. "I can't put in anything about you if you won't talk to me."

Black Eagle lingered and talked until daylight, his boycott ended.

Knowing about the Indians' spiritual beliefs, Edward once was able to make use of a timely stroke of the elements to help him gain the information he wanted. He had ridden his horse for hours through a cold rain to get the story of a certain sacred ceremony from an old priest who had promised to reveal the whole secret. The priest hadn't gone far with his story, however, when Edward realized, from the translations of his interpreter, that the priest was leaving out the most important parts of the account.

Edward held up his hand in protest. "Your gods will be angry because you lied to me," he said. A flash of lightning rent the sky, followed by a thunderclap which reverberated loudly.

"See," Edward said, "they are angry. They know you haven't told me the truth."

The priest quickly climbed to the roof of the lodge. There he waved his sacred white buffalo robe at the heavens and as the storm increased, appealed to the gods to forgive him, his voice frequently lost in peals of thunder. When the storm waned, indicating that his transgression had been forgiven, the priest returned to the ground and gave Edward the story in full.

From experience Edward learned that the key to winning the Indians' confidence was religion. If he could get them to talk about this, a profoundly private matter with them, the rest was easy. But to get them to open up about religion called for extreme patience.

"Even the cultivated man of civilization is loathe to open the inner sanctum of his soul to the inquisitive," Edward pointed out to an interviewer. "If educated people object to such self-exhibition, what can be expected of the primitive man who from the first has been told that his gods are fictitious, and that his superstitions . . . are wrong and childish?" he asked.

"Every act of their lives is influenced or regulated in some way by their religion or superstitions," Edward went on, "and their rituals are all accompanied by prayer. To the question, 'What are the words of that prayer?', the priest will often answer, 'It is a prayer too sacred to say in words. We only think of that prayer.' "

To qualify himself to discuss religion with the Indians, Edward made a study of religion in general, learning about the many forms it has taken among diverse people at different times throughout man's history. He built up a sizeable library on the subject, which he kept to the end of his life.

If, with this preparation, he still found an answer slow to come, Edward would say something which he knew was incorrect, either about the religion of the Indians he was with or that of another tribe.

"That's wrong," the Indian would say. "Here's the way it is," and the talk would be underway.

Because of his knowledgeability in religion, the Indians felt that in Edward they had a friend who understood with them what Chief Black Elk of the Oglala Sioux was saying in his prayer: "We should understand well that all things are the works of the Great Spirit. We should know that He is within all things—the trees, the grasses, the rivers, the mountains, and all the four-legged animals, and the winged peoples; and even more important we should understand all this deeply in our hearts, then we will fear, and love, and know the Great Spirit, and then we will be and act and live as He intends."

3. Pictures Which Will Live for All Time

"The White House," read the envelope—"Personal." With unsteady fingers, Edward tore it open. The letter was from President Theodore Roosevelt, who as vice president had succeeded to the presidency after the assassination of William McKinley in 1901.

In his letter the President invited Edward to visit Sagamore Hill, the Roosevelt summer home, at Oyster Bay, New York, and take pictures of the Roosevelt family. TR, as he was popularly known, knew about the quality of Edward's work from having seen his photographs in the Most-Beautiful-Girl-in-America Contest, published in the *Ladies' Home Journal.*

Eagerly fitting the President's invitation into his schedule for the summer, Edward brought along a folder of his Indian pictures to show him. He knew that Roosevelt had lived a number of years on his Elkhorn Ranch in the Dakota Badlands, in the heart of Indian country, and as an author as well as politician, had written sympathetically about the Indians. Roosevelt's four-volume work, *The Winning of the West,* had been a best seller.

Roosevelt admiringly examined each of Edward's photographs as Edward described what he had set out to do.

"This is a very worthy undertaking," TR said with emphasis. "No man could be doing anything more important. I will support you in any way I can."

Greatly encouraged by this response from the President of the

Theodore Roosevelt photographed by Edward Curtis

United States, Edward returned to the field with his camera, visiting the Navahos, Apaches, and Jicarillas, in the Southwest. At the finish of the visit, lasting into October of 1904, Edward wrote of his growing enthusiasm to Edward Webb Hodge, well-known Indian authority, at the Bureau of Ethnology of the Smithsonian Institution in Washington, D.C. "The longer I work at this collection of pictures, the more certain I feel of their great value."

But, at the same time, something worried him. "The only question now, in my mind, is, will I be able to keep at the thing long enough . . . as doing it in a thorough way is enormously expensive," he wrote, "and I am finding it rather difficult to give as much time to the work as I would like."

41

The Three Chiefs—Piegan

The Vanishing Race—Navaho

In December, friends of Edward's in Seattle hired Christensen's Hall, so he could show the public what he had, hoping this would stimulate sales of his prints. The hall was packed and the show a hit. A particular favorite with the audience was *The Three Chiefs*, showing three Indian horsemen on the plain scanning the horizon. "This picture is so remarkable in its lines of composition that we marvel how the artistic requirements could be accomplished with the camera," commented the Seattle *Times*.

Another favorite was *The Vanishing Race*, a column of Indians on horseback fading into the shadows at twilight. This photograph "with its ghostly figures," had "a haunting mysticism rarely found in pictures," the *Times* wrote.

This was especially gratifying to Edward; he had been afraid the picture of the retiring riders might be too dark when he brought the plate to the studio to be developed.

Not long after he had been given this reception at Christensen's Hall, Edward was guest of honor at the exclusive Rainier Club, where he entranced his audience as he showed them 150 of his lantern slides, converted from his negatives, telling the story behind each picture. "The club learned for the first time the real meaning of the Curtis Indians," the Seattle *Times* reported.

When news accounts of the Rainier Club event reached Portland, Oregon, Edward was invited to come there and put on his show. Again, he delighted his viewers. "The touch of the artist is everywhere visible," the Portland *Oregonian* wrote. "Even the skies seem to bend to the will of his genius. His marvelous portraits of Indians [are] an educational work of unique and remarkable value which should be enjoyed by all public school pupils, teachers, students of American history and the public generally."

The newspaper approvingly noted that a new term had been coined for Edward: "Photo-historian."

Taking a cue from his western audiences, Edward packed up a careful selection of his pictures and took them to Washington, D.C. There, with the help of his old friend, E. H. Harriman, who knew his work

43

well from the expedition to Alaska in 1900, he arranged for an exhibit of his photographs at the fashionable Washington Club, whose members had wealth and influence.

This led to a second exhibit, at the equally select Cosmos Club, housed at the historic home of Dolly Madison, wife of President James Madison. Both exhibits brought lavish praise.

Gifford Pinchot, one of the men Edward met on the glacier that night a half-dozen years before and still chief of the Division of Forestry, invited Edward to his home for dinner and to show his photographs. "I certainly have seen no such collection anywhere in the world," Pinchot exclaimed.

In addition, while he was in town, Edward was invited to address the National Academy of Sciences—no small honor for a man whose formal education ended in a one-room schoolhouse.

It happened also while he was in Washington that an historic event was taking place: Theodore Roosevelt, elected to his own term by a landslide and destined to become the most popular president since Abraham Lincoln, was being inaugurated on March 4, 1904. Francis Leupp, Commissioner of Indian Affairs, asked Edward to photograph a group of Indian chiefs invited to the city to ride in the inaugural parade.

A light rain was falling, and as Edward approached the White House lawn to set up his tripod, an Indian smiled and opened the red blanket he was wearing and enfolded Edward within it, the two then walking forward together. The Indian was Geronimo, the famous chief of the Apaches, onetime terror of the plains. He now lived the quiet life of a farmer at Fort Sill, Oklahoma, built in the late 1860s as one of the forts to keep watch on the Indians.

From Washington, Edward went to New York and exhibited his photographs in the grand ballroom of the Waldorf-Astoria, a favorite haunt of the city's socially elite families called the 400. They turned out in force to see the pictures by the young man from Seattle, among them Mrs. Jay Gould, wife of E. H. Harriman's chief rival in building

Geronimo—Apache

44

and buying railroads; Mrs. Frederick K. Vanderbilt, of the family that owned steamship lines as well as railroads; and Mrs. Douglas Robinson, sister of President Roosevelt.

Happily for Edward, the visitors did more than look at his photographs. To his vast relief, they also bought them, enabling him to pay the $1,300 it cost to rent the hall.

At the close of the Waldorf show, Edward shipped his pictures back across the continent and put them on display at the Lewis and Clark Fair at Portland, Oregon, with results by now pleasantly familiar.

"The present day life of every people in this big world is shown," the Portland *Oregonian* wrote admiringly of the fair. "The arts and crafts of the Orientals, the equally admirable arts and crafts of the Americans, the almost unbelievable progress in mechanical arts, and the heart story of Mother Earth, laid bare in the richness of the minerals and agricultural products, which are here for the inspection of the visitor. But the exhibit which will mean more than any other to the American and his history a thousand years from now is a little group of Indian photographs which occupies a quiet corner in the attic of the forestry building.

" 'The Story of a Vanishing Race' is told in these pictures by E. S. Curtis, who is an artist, photographer, historian, explorer, and ethnologist. . . . It is a series of pictures which will live for all time."

The newspaper went on to say that no better setting to show "these rare pictures" could have been found than the forestry building. "From the corner high up among the rafters, where they hang against the bark of the giant logs, one looks down through the columns of colossal timbers which support the building and wonders—and dreams," the paper observed. "Perhaps some of the pictured red men on the wall rode through the primeval forest from which these monster trees were taken by the white invaders—perhaps a tepee stood under that tree or a brave stood behind this one waiting for wild game or the hated paleface. Another glance at the pictures and it is hard to believe that it was not the whisk of a war bonnet down through the shady isle a hundred feet below. But, after all, they are just Curtis' Indian pictures in Nature's setting."

46

During his stay east in 1905, Edward had the further satisfaction of reading a glowing piece about himself and his work in a national publication for the first time. This was an article by his friend George Bird Grinnell in the respected and widely read *Scribner's Magazine*.

"It is easy to conceive that if Curtis shall have his health . . . he will then have accumulated material for the greatest artistic and historical work in American ethnology that has ever been conceived of," Grinnell wrote. "I have never seen pictures relating to Indians which, for fidelity to nature, combined with artistic feeling, can compare with these. . . ."

Vash Gon—*Jicarilla*

More than most, Grinnell appreciated what Edward had gone through to get these results. ". . . He has exchanged ease, comfort, home life, for the hardest kind of work, frequent and long-continued separation from his family, the wearing toil of travel through difficult regions, and finally the heart-breaking struggle of winning over to his purpose primitive men, to whom ambition, time and money mean nothing, but to whom a dream or a cloud in the sky, or a bird flying across the trail from the wrong direction, means much."

The reward of fine words for his work, if not of much money, at

Red Cloud—
Ogalala

least kept Edward's spirits up and he struggled on. As the summer of 1905 began, he traveled to South Dakota to visit the Sioux, one of the last tribes to surrender to the white man. With Chief Red Hawk and twenty of the chief's followers riding with him, starting at Wounded Knee, he explored the Dakota Badlands, some fifty miles to the north.

The Badlands, a place of grotesque scenery caused by erosion and of fossil remains from millions of years ago, were sacred to the Sioux. The Indians objected when the white man, finding gold in the region, trespassed on these holy grounds in violation of his treaty with the Sioux respecting the Badlands as theirs.

The troubles thus invited by the white man climaxed with the Battle of the Little Bighorn in 1876, when General George Armstrong Custer and his entire command were wiped out to the last man by the Sioux under Sitting Bull. Then came that cold December day, fourteen years later, when the United States Cavalry, in an act of berserk savagery repeated many times since the white man began his push across the plains, vengefully slaughtered 300 captive Indians at Wounded Knee, most of them old men, women, and children, all but ending the red man's resistance to the encroachments of the whites.

It was during his jaunt to the Badlands that Edward made one of his best-known pictures. This was *An Oasis in the Bad Lands,* showing Chief Red Hawk watering his horse at a prairie water hole.

As he ended his visit among the Sioux, Edward told Red Hawk "I'm coming back to see you. Then I'm going to give you and the men who rode with us to the Badlands a feast."

Red Hawk was pleased. In return, he promised to set up an old-time Sioux camp and have his followers go through some of the tribe's ancient ceremonies for Edward's camera. There would be no clothing or other trace of the white man showing—all would be as it was before the Sioux ever heard of the paleface.

That same summer, at Nespelem, Washington, Edward helped to rebury a friend whose passing had been a jarring reminder that the past which Red Hawk would help him recapture was steadily slipping farther away and there was need to work fast—before there was no one left to remember it. The friend was Chief Joseph, leader of the Nez Percé tribe.

Edward had spent much time with Joseph, considered by many the greatest Indian of them all, getting from his own lips the story of betrayal and brutality dealt him and his tribe by the whites. Joseph had died the previous autumn—of a broken heart, the doctor said— and was buried in a temporary grave while the Washington University State Historical Society prepared a monument for him.

The shaft was of white marble and stood seven-and-a-half feet high. The front bore a carved likeness of Joseph, with "Chief Joseph" in raised letters beneath. On another side appeared his Indian name, along with its English translation, "Thunder Rolling in the Mountains."

An Oasis in the Bad Lands

Edward did most of the digging, he remembered nearly half a century later. To Harriet Leitch of the Seattle Public Library, who had asked him for information about his own life, he wrote, "It was a very hot day and the Noble Red Men said, 'Let the white men do the digging. They know how.'"

By the end of 1905, Edward's need for financial help had become acute. The money brought in from the sale of his photographs fell far short of what he needed. The income from his studio in Seattle all went to keep his family. He faced the grim prospect of having to give up his project.

51

4. I Want to See These Photographs in Books

Snow and sleet driven by a prairie gale stung the windows of the car as Edward's train rolled eastward on a January day in 1906. The mournful, far-off sound of the whistle up in front did nothing to lift his sagging spirits as he pondered what he might do to keep his work going.

He remembered that he had an influential friend at the White House. Hadn't TR promised to support Edward's work any way he could when Edward was a guest at the Roosevelt summer home to photograph the family a year and a half before? Edward knew the President had not spoken idly. By the time he reached New York, he had the words well in mind and he wrote the President a letter, asking for a testimonial which he could use in trying to raise funds.

The President responded with a letter addressed "To Whom It May Concern," praising Edward's work and saying how important it was. Use this "in talking with any man who has an interest in the subject," he wrote.

Possibly one such man, Edward thought, was J. Pierpont Morgan. He knew that Morgan, besides being a man of great wealth, also was a philanthropist, generously supporting the arts and other cultural causes he believed in. Edward arranged to see Morgan—how, is not known, but presumably with the help of his letter from the President.

Enthroned behind his huge teakwood desk, the King of Wall Street listened without expression as Edward nervously told his story.

J. Pierpont Morgan

"Mr. Curtis," Morgan is said to have interrupted, "there are many demands on me for financial assistance. I will be unable to help you."

Edward opened his portfolio, took out a photograph, and placed it in front of Morgan, who looked at it. Edward put another before him. He kept the pictures coming, one by one, until all were on the desk, under the eyes of the man who held Edward's future in his hands. Morgan examined each photograph thoughtfully.

"Mr. Curtis," he said at length, "I want to see these photographs in books—the most beautiful set of books ever published."

He wanted writing to go with the pictures, telling the Indians' customs, ceremonials, beliefs, myths, what they did day to day. Edward

Edward S. Curtis

finally would develop a list of twenty-five areas of information about
the Indians to explore.

Books—with text? Edward had never thought of that, only pictures
with descriptive titles. "Who would do the writing?" he asked.

Morgan fixed Edward with that penetrating eye for which he was
known, and replied at once. "You know the Indians and how they live
and what they think. You are the one to write it."

The plan decided on called for the work to be published in twenty
volumes, each book accompanied by a portfolio of prints from the
photographs, in a limited edition of 500 sets. Two kinds of paper were
to be used, both handmade imports and the most expensive to be had:
Japanese vellum and a paper from Holland called Van Gelder. The

54

price was eventually fixed at $3,000 for the set printed on vellum, $3,850 for the other. These prices, Morgan estimated, would more than meet the cost of publishing the books.

Morgan agreed to help with Edward's expenses in the field, putting up $75,000, to be paid out at the rate of $15,000 a year for five years. In return, Morgan would receive twenty-five of the $3,000 sets, plus the matching portfolios of prints.

Once the project had grown to include text as well as pictures, it was decided to go yet another step—to capture the music and language of the Indians by wax cylinder recorder. First shown to the public by inventor Thomas A. Edison in 1878, this mechanism had little in common with today's tape recorder. The sound was etched by needle on a wax-coated cylinder about the size of a water tumbler, and it was very cumbersome and complicated—but it worked.

The recording part of Edward's project grew to become larger than anything of the kind ever undertaken before. "In the coastal states of California and Oregon," he wrote later, "we recorded more root languages than exist on the face of the globe. In several cases, we collected and recorded the vocabularies from the last living man knowing the words of a root language."

Altogether, they recorded 75 languages and more than 10,000 songs, in addition to taking more than 40,000 pictures—covering 80 tribes from the Mexican border to Alaska.

To edit his writing from the field, Edward chose Frederick Webb Hodge at the Smithsonian Institution in Washington, D.C. Dr. Hodge probably knew as much about the North American Indian as any man alive. He had been with the Institution's Bureau of Ethnology since 1889 and led many of its expeditions to the Southwest to study Indians. He edited *The American Anthropologist*, published periodically, as well as many historical source narratives dealing with the Southwest. At the time he agreed to edit Edward's work, at seven dollars a thousand words, he was working on a 1,300-page, two-volume work for the Bureau of Ethnology: *Handbook of the American Indian*.

Having gotten his money problem at least temporarily settled, and

Frederick Webb Hodge

with the project much expanded, Edward was anxious to get back to the field. He delayed his departure to photograph the wedding of President Roosevelt's daughter, Alice, to New York Congressman Nicholas Longworth, the top social event of the season, on February 17. Then he prepared to head west.

As always, Edward planned his work carefully. "Will you please write me in the next few weeks, addressed to Seattle, as to any points which I may take up in the White Mountain Apache country," he wrote to Hodge from the Waldorf-Astoria on March 26. "Also, if you know of an available map there in Washington which gives a good detail of that country, I wish you would have a copy mailed to me. Something on which I can check up the primitive home location of the different bands.

56

"I shall write you from time to time and tell you how matters are going and perhaps ask you a few questions in regard to points on which I am not certain."

Arriving in Seattle, Edward found there was still something he needed from Hodge. "Once more I must bother you," he wrote, "but if you have a copy of your paper, 'The Early Navaho and Apache,' will you please send me one?" He added in passing, "I am a little upset with the California calamity, and slightly delayed as part of my equipment was there and must be replaced."

The "California calamity" was the historic earthquake which struck San Francisco in 1906, killing 600 people and leaving 300,000 homeless. How close Edward had come to being one of the victims there is no telling. Had he left his equipment there as he passed through on his way to Seattle, to be picked up as he returned through the city en route to the Apache country in the southwest? He had left the East just seven days before the disaster, which would have placed him within hours of San Francisco when the earthquake hit—if in fact he passed that way.

It was typical of Edward that he said nothing about these things in his letter to Hodge. He was "one of the most genial and pleasant of men," once wrote A. F. Muhr, employee of Edward's Seattle studio, but he had no time to waste on misadventure, except as he felt he had to—like the time he came in from the field with his camera "held together by a rope tied in a diamond cinch about it, and when this was untied the camera fell apart." His mule had fallen off a cliff, carrying the camera with it, Edward had briefly explained.

By early June, earthquakes notwithstanding, Edward was in Apacheland, eager to pick up where he had left off months before. "We are here in the Apache country, working away the best we can," he wrote Hodge from the town of Holbrook, Arizona. "I feel certain we are going to be very successful in getting a lot of splendid Apache material. Perhaps the least bit too certain of it—however, I know it's going to be a very successful effort . . . one thing is certain, at the time I quit the Apache Reservation, there will be a good many questions answered as to the inner life of the Apache. . . ."

If Edward could make good on this, he would have succeeded where all others had failed. The Apache guarded the secrets of his religion so closely that, taken together with his supposed ferocity, many believed he didn't have any.

"I realized it would require the greatest skill and patience on my part," Edward wrote in the memoirs which he briefly undertook near the end of his life. He had begun by pretending great indifference as he approached them. "I asked no questions and indicated no special interest in more than casual things."

It did not take him long to discover that the Apache was, in fact, deeply religious. All he had to do to find out was to keep his eyes and ears open as the Indians went about the routines of the day from morning to night.

"The men rose at dawn and bathed in pools or streams that their bodies be acceptable to the gods," he wrote. "Each man in isolation greeted the rising sun in fervent prayer. Secretly shrines were visited and invocations made. I realized, though, if I asked a single question or displayed any curiosity as to their devotional rites, I would defeat my purpose."

After a time, as he went on pretending disinterest, the Apaches invited Edward to go along on their annual trip into the mountains to harvest mescal, an important food for them. Also known as the century plant, mescal is a kind of cactus. The edible part is the root, which, when it is trimmed, somewhat resembles a head of cabbage and weighs five to twenty pounds. Mescal is also a source of intoxicants, used in religious rites by the Apaches.

"That first night, with Indian courtesy," Edward wrote, "they allowed me to pick my camp site first, which I chose by the river under the shade of a walnut tree. Around the campfire that evening we sat telling stories."

Edward thought this might be the time to start feeling them out about their religion. He tried to lead the conversation in this direction, but his tactics failed. "While they talked of the mescal harvest, I tried to learn the Apache story of its origin, but of that they were noncommittal. Their Indian life was not for a white man to know."

Many days later, when the mescal had been gathered and brought to the cooking pit, Edward listened closely to the ritual which attended the lighting of the fire under the mescal. "In their prayers I heard the names of the divine ones constantly repeated until I, too, knew the names of the gods of the east, west, north, and south, the sky and the earth," he wrote.

But it was still all a mystery to him. "I had no key to this vast storehouse of primitive thought," he went on. "At least I had excellent pictures of the entire harvest and ceremony."

Back at the village when the mescal harvest was over, Edward stayed on with his Apache hosts, still acting as if he had no special interest in them, but continually listening and watching for clues to what he was after. After many months he left, knowing little more about the Apaches' religious life than when he came.

The Storm—Apache

The following season, after concluding a visit to Washington, Edward was ready to try again. As he prepared to leave, he told an Indian "expert" of high standing of his eagerness to get back to the Southwest and dig out the secrets of the Apaches' religion. "In all my travels among the Indians, I've known none who were more close-mouthed about it," Edward said.

The other raised his eyebrows and looked askance at him. "Don't you realize you are trying to get something that doesn't exist?" he replied haughtily. "The Apache has no religion."

"How do you know?" Edward asked, taken aback that a man of science had closed his mind on a matter before it had been thoroughly investigated.

"I spent considerable time among them and they told me they had

Jicarilla Maiden

no religion," the expert answered. "You're wasting your time."

Edward left Washington more determined than ever to bring back proof of what he already knew to be true: that the Apache was one of the most religious of Indians.

Arriving back among them with his assistants, Edward was greeted like an old friend. This encouraged him to broach the question uppermost in his mind, without waiting.

Like a sudden shift in the weather, the atmosphere changed instantly. "Old friends looked the other way," Edward wrote. "One of my former interpreters declined to have anything to do with me, declaring he was not going in search of sudden death."

Edward tried subtle bribery. It got him nothing. "At the end of six weeks of patient work we had succeeded only in building up a wall of tribal reticence," he wrote. "Every member of the tribe understood that no one was to talk to us and a delegation of the chiefs had visited the Indian agent in charge, demanding that I leave the reservation."

Edward kept trying. "With the greatest stealth, I approached several of the medicine men in an effort to secure even a key to the situation," he went on. "A few words of information would serve as a leverage to learning more. I managed to speak with several of the foremost medicine men, but on the subject of religion they were as silent as the Sphinx."

A medicine man, Edward knew, was more than a doctor. He was a seer and a prophet as well, sometimes trained from infancy. While he was usually not a priest, he was considered to have supernatural powers, as over illness and the weather. He was a man of special gifts and influence; he would know all about a tribe's religion.

Somehow, as he persevered, Edward was able to learn that there was a split among the tribe's medicine men. Perhaps he might turn this situation to his advantage. One medicine man was Das-lan, who was ambitiously promoting a new cult which he claimed had been revealed to him by the gods. "This crafty medicine man hoped to supplant Gosh-o-ne, the present high priest," Edward wrote.

Edward tried a number of times to talk to Gosh-o-ne, but was always rebuffed. Still, the priest seemed friendly. The interpreter confided that the old man felt strongly about Das-lan, considering him an upstart, and believed he might finally talk to Edward. He advised him to make the approach once more.

Walking at night, Edward and his assistants reached Gosh-o-ne's camp at daybreak. "In concealment we watched the old priest emerge for his morning prayer to the sun," Edward wrote. "At the close of his invocation we approached and once more made our plea that he tell us how the world began.

"Without protest or comment, he said, 'I think I will tell you that story.' Then he led us to a secluded spot among the shrubbery at the brookside. First he invoked the sun in short prayer. Then without prelude he began the story of the gods and the creation of the earth and its people."

Gosh-o-ne talked until noon, pouring out a story for his spellbound listeners never before heard by a white man. "That is how we learned

the Apache Creation Myth," Edward wrote. "In poetry of imagination I believe it supreme in genetic legends from the American Indians."

There was more success for Edward. By what he called "a miracle," he was able to lay hands on one of the most sacred objects owned by the Apaches. This was a medicine man's prayer chart, complete with a full description of all its symbols.

"Such a chart without the description would only be interesting primitive art, but learning the functions of every character represented by figure or symbol, it became a document beyond price," he wrote. "To us its greatest interest was the fact that its description confirmed in every detail the information secured from Gosh-o-ne."

Prayer charts or, as the Apaches called them, medicine charts, were painted on deerskin by the medicine men themselves, each man according to his own private guidance from the gods. "The one I obtained was considered the most important and potent in existence and no white

Above: Sacred Buckskin—Apache
Left: Apache Medicine-man

Cañon de Chelly—
Navaho

man had ever been allowed to see it," Edward added. How he obtained the prayer chart, Edward kept to himself, a secret between him and the Apaches.

Finished with the Apaches, Edward moved on to their neighbors, the Navahos. These lived in Canyon de Chelly, a spectacular thirty-mile-long gash in the earth enclosed by towering, water-streaked walls of red sandstone ranging up to a thousand feet high, in the northeast corner of Arizona.

It was here that the Navahos, living by agriculture, made their last losing stand against the white man less than fifty years earlier. Their immediate enemy was the legendary Kit Carson, a five-foot, six-inch little giant in buckskin who became the hero and inspiration of American boyhood. Like Edward, Carson was a friend of the Indians, and it was with reluctance that, as a colonel in the Army, he carried out orders to burn the crops and kill the animals of the Navahos in Canyon de Chelly.

However he felt about it privately, Colonel Carson fulfilled his assignment with diabolical efficiency. When he finished with fire, bullet, and ax, nothing lived in Canyon de Chelly for the Navahos. All was death and ashes, including what they loved and prided themselves in most—more than 5,000 peach trees.

With this background, the Navahos held added interest for Edward as he prepared to visit them in the summer of 1906. He saw little of his family; school was out. He decided this was an ideal time to have them join him in the field for the next several weeks, sharing with him the remarkable surroundings of Canyon de Chelly.

With his four-horse covered wagon, he met them at Gallup, New Mexico, fifty miles or so to the southeast from the canyon. It was a happy, excited group that got off the train from Seattle. Edward's wife and three wide-eyed youngsters—Harold, eleven; Beth, nine; and Florence, seven—would all be seeing for the first time what life was like for their father.

They camped the first night at St. Michael's, just over the line in Arizona and not far from Fort Defiance, the first fort built in Navaho

Florence, Harold, and Beth with their mother, Clara Curtis

country by the whites and where Kit Carson was based when he rode against the Indians. Next morning, while the children watched a Navaho woman weaving a rug under a cottonwood tree, Edward loaded up with supplies at Day's Trading Post.

This was run by Sam Day who, with his wife, a schoolteacher, had come here as a civil engineer for the government to survey the boundaries for the Navaho reservation, but had liked the country so much he stayed. Charlie Day, one of the Day's two sons who had grown up with Indian boys for playmates, became Edward's interpreter and guide.

Edward had the horses hitched to the wagon and was at the point

The Blanket Weaver—Navaho

of moving out when a flash flood burst thunderously down on the camp, the product of a rainstorm somewhere in the distant mountains.

"Look out!" Edward cried, as he saw the wall of water, "Run!"

Clara and the children raced for higher ground, while Edward scrambled to save his equipment, water swirling around his waist. Happily, he had long since learned to pack his photo supplies and other critical items in waterproof containers.

The red walls of Canyon de Chelly rose gradually out of the plain, growing higher on each side of the wagon until they seemed to touch the blue of the sky far above. Edward made camp in a grove of cottonwoods. As he went about his work with his camera, the children savored the enchantments of a world no school book had yet prepared them for.

"They were idyllic days," Florence remembered. "We had a burro to ride—sometimes all three of us astride his back. We loved him but not his raucous hee-haw that echoed and re-echoed through the canyon. We made the acquaintance for the first time of horned toads, and my sister and I found they made great pets."

They explored cliff dwellings, where ancestors of the Navahos had lived thousands of years ago. "The Indians permitted it if we did not desecrate the dwellings of the 'old ones,' " Florence said. "Father had added his strict admonition in his quiet way and we sensed its importance."

All at once the canyon became strangely quiet and deserted. "No Indians were to be seen," Florence said. "We were given strict orders not to leave camp. The quiet was broken only by the chanting of medicine men, which echoed and reverberated until it became a ceaseless sound in the canyon."

It was years before the youngsters learned what was going on. "An Indian mother was giving birth, and it was proving most difficult.

Florence at Canyon de Chelly in 1906

Medicine men were called, and they attributed her complications to the fact that white people were camped nearby. Hour after hour, night following day, the canyon echoed with that eerie, gruesome chant."

Matters came to a climax when Edward and Charlie Day galloped into camp. "Tents and equipment were hastily thrown into the wagon; the horses were hitched and in the greatest haste we started out." Progress was slow as the wheels sank into the sands of the canyon floor, and the horses were lashed to extra effort.

Why they were leaving now—and hadn't left sooner—Florence also learned in time. Charlie Day had told her father, "You dare not leave until the baby is born." And now that the child had arrived, Charlie had a further injunction. "Pray that the baby will live for there is no power on earth that will save you and your family if it should die."

Edward admitted to Florence long after that in all the years he worked among Indians, he had never been more frightened. "I knew I was completely helpless to save my family," he said. "Their lives hung on the whim of the medicine men. I vowed then that never again would I include all the family on a trip into Indian country."

Charlie Day, Edward, Florence, Beth, and a Navaho

A Chief of the Desert

Aside from things going wrong in Canyon de Chelly, the year 1906 was a good one for Edward. In September he wrote to Hodge, "I have my material for the first volume of the Apache Navajo nearly completed and the photogravure people are working on the first lot of plates. . . . I feel that everything is in splendid shape and progressing rapidly.

"One question I would like to ask. I have, in thinking of a title for the book, thought of the following title, 'The North American Indian.' The only question seemed to me to be, has this title been used before. Will you tell me what you think of it."

The field work done, Edward shut himself away in a cabin on

A Son of the Desert—Navaho

Puget Sound which the family had built the year before, to make his summer's work ready for publication. With him were his assistants—Edmond Schwinke, W. E. Myers, and William Phillips.

For three months the four men toiled without the distraction of a newspaper, from eight o'clock in the morning until one the next, seven days a week. At long intervals one of their number slipped out to check the post office for mail.

On the day they were through, Phillips left for the East with the manuscript, to stay there and look after its publication. Edward followed shortly, to make sure there was no delay in getting the material into Hodge's hands for his first job of editing.

"I am now sending you by express the first two volumes," Edward wrote Hodge from New York on March 27, 1907.

The North American Indian was on its way.

72

Qahátika *Girl*

5. They Question Your Work

The President came straight to the point. "I have had a complaint from a professor at Columbia University," he began bluntly. "Because you do not have a formal degree in ethnological research they question the validity of your work. There is only one answer. I have appointed a committee of three men whom I consider supreme authorities in our country to go over your work and render a decision." He paused. "I am sure you know how I personally feel about this."

Edward was stunned. When TR had called him to the White House, he had not suspected anything like this. Someone was saying that because he had not gone to school as much as some men, he was unfit to do what he was doing. He was grateful that the President took a less narrow view of the issue and had taken steps to let Edward's work speak for itself.

The men Roosevelt had named to be his judges were indeed giants in their respective fields: Henry Fairfield Osborn, curator of vertebrate paleontology at the American Museum of Natural History, New York; William Henry Holmes, chief of the Bureau of Ethnology at the Smithsonian Institution, Dr. Hodge's superior; and Charles Doolittle Walcott, secretary of the Smithsonian.

Of equal stature was the man who had raised the question of Edward's qualifications. He was Dr. Franz Boaz, Columbia University's first professor of anthropology and one of the first anthropologists to spend any length of time in the field, as Edward was doing. For four years, Professor Boaz was curator of anthropology at the American Museum of

Natural History. He was an authority on the Indians and had written a great deal about certain tribes.

Edward turned over suitcases full of notebooks to these men, along with his Edison recordings and whatever else he had at hand which might be helpful. They were quick to ease his suspense. In a letter from Dr. Osborn, they not only approved his work but declared it outstanding. The crisis was over.

The episode had cost Edward a great deal of time, not to mention some sleepless nights. Ready at last to return to the field, he wrote Hodge, "My field address for a few weeks will be Pine Ridge, South Dakota. Any special thought that occurs to you that I should follow in the Sioux or Northern Plains work I shall be very glad to have. Mr. Myers has been at work at Pine Ridge and writes me that everything is moving along very well."

W. E. Myers was Edward's good right hand. Myers was a master of shorthand, a fast typist, an expert in spelling, and remarkably gifted as a phonetist.

"To the Indians his skill in phonetics was awesome magic," Edward wrote to Harriet Leitch of the Seattle Public Library near the end of his life. "An old informant would pronounce a seven-syllable word and Myers would repeat it without a second's hesitation, which to the old Indian was magic—and so it was to me. We might spend the early part of the night listening to the Indian dance songs, and as we walked back to camp Myers would sing them."

Edward described how they worked. "Most times . . . Myers sat at my left and the interpreter at my right. I led in asking questions and Myers and the interpreter prompted me if I overlooked any important points. . . .

"By writing all information in shorthand, we speeded the work to the utmost. I hazard the statement that our trio could do more work in a year than a lone investigator, writing in longhand and lacking phonetic skill could do in five years. Also, we knew nothing of labor union hours. Myers neatly typed his day's collection before going to bed. In that way field notes were kept up to the minute. Our average working time for a six month season would exceed sixteen hours per day."

If Myers needed to know more as he typed up his notes, he had only to dig into a small metal trunk filled with books about the tribe they were working with. It was largely the contents of Myers' notebooks which made short work of the questions raised by Franz Boaz.

While Myers baffled the Indians by his ability to repeat what they said or sang, this was nothing compared to their puzzlement at the machine that did the same thing—the Edison recorder. "The singers and fellow tribesmen were awe-struck on hearing the song as repeated from what they called the magic box," Edward wrote.

When Edward reached his camp at Pine Ridge, he found his wife and thirteen-year-old son Harold waiting for him. They had come up overland from the train at Fort Alliance, Nebraska, traveling by four-horse wagon, the usual off-road vehicle of the day, and would be spending the summer with him.

Edward found a horse for Harold and, leaving Clara behind at Pine Ridge to keep camp, they rode across the prairie from Pine Ridge to Wounded Knee Creek, about twenty miles northwest of Pine Ridge. For young Harold the ride was high adventure, to be remembered all his life. "The horses kept shying at the rattlesnakes in the grass," he recalled. "All along we saw cattle that were sick and with badly swollen heads from snake bite."

Edward had come back to Wounded Knee to keep his promise of two years earlier, in 1905, to give a feast to Chief Red Hawk and the other Sioux who had ridden with him on his visit to the Badlands that summer, in return for which the Indians would set up some scenes for Edward's camera.

The Indians had prepared for him, but there were a good many more on hand than the 20 who had been along on the ride to the Badlands. There appeared to be 300 or more. Chief Red Hawk had lost control of the occasion.

The welcoming ceremonies were well underway, with Edward reading letters from the Great Father, President Roosevelt, and from Indian

76

Commissioner Leupp, when Chief Iron Crow, who outranked Red Hawk, interrupted the proceedings. Waving for the interpreter, he pointed out that while there were 300 Indians present, only two beefs had been provided. "This isn't going to be enough," he said. He suggested that four beefs would be closer to what was needed.

"Chief Iron Crow is right," Edward tactfully agreed. "There will be more beef."

This brought many Hows and much handshaking, and the formalities went smoothly forward to the end. Next morning, however, as the Indians were about to start their first procession for Edward's camera, Chief Slow Bull held up a hand. He, too, wanted more beef, no less than Iron Crow.

"Slow Bull shall have more beef," Edward promised.

The action was about to begin, when for no apparent reason, the Indians suddenly decided to rest and smoke for the rest of the day. Red Hawk protested, but no one paid any attention to him. Edward quietly folded his camera, took down his tripod, and strode from the scene. He said nothing.

Red Hawk apparently regained control during the night, for in the morning he and Slow Bull rode into camp leading a column of warriors made up as in days gone by. The Indians restaged old battles, went through ancient rites, and retold the old stories. Edward busily photographed and recorded it all.

While he was at Pine Ridge, Edward made a trip up to the Little Bighorn battlefield in Montana, where in 1876 the Sioux disastrously defeated General George Armstrong Custer, killing all 264 men of his command as well as Custer himself. Edward wanted to see the place with his own eyes and hear with his own ears what had happened.

For days he rode back and forth across the scene of the battle, accompanied by three Crow Indians—White Man Runs Him, Goes Ahead, and Hairy Moccasins—who had scouted for Custer. The Crow tribe were enemies of the Sioux, who had once driven them from their hunting grounds.

When he had heard the story from the Crows as they saw it from

On the Little Bighorn—Apsaroke

Custer's side, Edward went over the ground again, this time with Chief Two Moon of the Cheyennes and a party of his warriors, who had fought on the side of their neighbors, the Sioux. Likewise riding with Edward was Chief Red Hawk, who remembered the battle in striking detail these twenty-one years later.

Finally, having heard the Indians' version of the battle on both sides, Edward rode over the battlefield with General Charles A. Woodruff and the three Crow scouts, so that an experienced Army officer could hear what they had to say. Still not satisfied, Edward spent hours listening to a group of Arikara scouts who, like the Crows, had been with Custer. Only then did he feel he knew the story.

Two Moons—Cheyenne

Back at Pine Ridge, Edward slowly won the Sioux confidence. Increasingly, they drifted into his camp to talk, confiding the secrets of the tribe. His tent was like a country store as the Indians lounged about outside, the older men favoring the shady side.

These scenes fascinated Professor Edmond S. Meany of the University of Washington, at one point a guest in Edward's camp. For years Professor Meany had spent his summers studying Indians, and he had never seen a white man get along with them as Edward did.

Meany had met "ethnologists, archaeologists, linguists, historians, and artists, but none of them seemed to come so close to the Indian" as Edward, he wrote in *World's Work*, March 1908. "So close that he seems a part of their life. . . . He will discuss religious topics with a group of old men; they will pass the pipe around the circle and say, 'he is just like us, he knows about the Great Mystery.'"

The Indians of the Sioux country that summer of 1907 became so relaxed toward Edward that they made mock attacks on his wagon as he traveled about among them, all intended to be entertaining. Edward would first see a small figure on a distant hill—an Indian scout. Then, as he approached, a band of Indians swooped down out of nowhere, riding their horses at breakneck speed, filling the air with blood-chilling yells.

As the Indians rode in close, the "attackers" slipped to the far side of their horses and let loose with their rifles, firing blanks from under the horse's belly and between his front legs, as well as over the top. Round and around the wagon they galloped, keeping up a fearful hullabaloo. Grimly, Edward hung on, waiting for the moment when his team bolted and broke from the harness. Then the circus ended.

As the summer passed, Edward found himself with a deeper concern on his hands. Harold became ill. The boy manfully said nothing about it until his father noticed him slumping in the saddle, so sick he was at the point of falling to the ground. He was laid out on a rubber mattress under a cottonwood tree, in the care of his mother who diagnosed the illness as typhoid fever; she had once nursed Edward through a siege of the same ailment.

The oath—Sioux

Curtis driving his team

There wasn't much she could do for Harold except try to keep his strength up, feeding him prairie chicken soup and catfish soup. Every few days Edward sent an Indian in a buckboard to the nearest railway whistle-stop, twenty miles away, to flag the next eastbound train and hand the conductor a prescription to be filled in Chicago. The train didn't always stop and it would be a week or more before Harold got his medicine.

Youth and basic good health finally won out, and Harold slowly started to recover. When he was strong enough to travel, his parents loaded him into the wagon, mattress and all, and drove to the whistle-stop. Luckily, the train screeched to a halt. The conductor helped lift

The Winter Camp—Sioux

A Heavy Load—Sioux

Harold aboard, making a place for his mattress by opening two seats. The cars jerked and Harold and his mother were on their way to Chicago, where his mother would find a Pullman for a more elegant passage back across the plains, home to Seattle.

As he picked up the reins and turned the wagon around to start back to Pine Ridge, Edward sighed with relief that the story hadn't ended tragically. Reaching his camp, he lost no time striking the tent and heading for North Dakota to join Myers, who had gone on ahead some time before to start work among the Mandan Indians. Harold's illness had put Edward a month behind schedule.

Already autumn hung subtly in the air.

6. The Sacred Turtles

There was snow on the ground and a cold wind whistling through the woods as Edward and Upshaw, his interpreter, rode up to Packs Wolf's cabin. They were on a mission to photograph the Sacred Turtles of the Mandans, used by the tribe in a number of key ceremonies.

The turtles, once live creatures but now replicas of buffalo hide, had never been seen by a white man. Edward was determined both to get pictures of these sacred objects and at the same time the legendary story behind them. This would be an accomplishment on a par with getting the prayer chart from the Apaches.

Aware it would take some time to make the arrangements, if they could be made at all, Edward had initiated the project during the summer.

"I entrusted negotiations with the Keeper of the Turtles to Upshaw, knowing it required an Indian mind to more ably win an Indian argument," Edward wrote in the memoirs which he never completed. "After many months, Upshaw reported that Packs Wolf, the Keeper of the Turtles, had consented to give us the information we wanted."

Packs Wolf directed Upshaw to come to his home early in the winter. He kept the Turtles in a log house near his own, he explained.

"Packs Wolf and two other medicine men, confederates in this unethical affair, were awaiting us," Edward wrote. "After warming our chilled bodies, it was explained that preparatory to going into the House of the Turtles, I must go through a sweat bath that my body would be purified and thus made acceptable to the Spirit People and the Turtles."

Edward described the sweat lodge as "a small, dome-shaped framework of willow wands covered with blankets, some distance from Packs Wolf's house, near the edge of a cliff. Close by was the fire for heating rocks."

Following instructions, Edward took off his clothes in a snowbank, and with the others entered the sweat lodge, seating himself beside the three medicine men and Upshaw. "We sat on our haunches with our backs to the blanket wall," he wrote. "Before us was a shallow pit into which an attendant dropped hot rocks. The blanket opening was lightly closed and the singing began."

From time to time, at certain words of the song, water was thrown on the rocks, filling the room with steam and causing Edward to forget "the chilling temperature outside." Upshaw had warned that the Indians would make things as hot as they could for him. "If it gets too hot," Upshaw had advised, "lower your head and raise an edge of the blanket for air, but don't do it unless you absolutely have to. It is not good form."

*Upshaw—
Apsaroke*

Edward didn't bother to explain that he had been through a few of these ordeals before—such as the Navaho Yebichai, a disease-curing ceremony in which the subject is sweated for four days. "The Indians seemed to enjoy giving a white man the best sweat possible," he wrote.

At the end of four songs, someone else lifted the blanket a little, saving Edward the trouble. The cold air felt delicious. A fresh batch of hot boulders was thrown into the fire pit, loosing new clouds of steam and setting the stage for more songs. By the fourth round of singing, the temperature was near the roasting point.

At this stage the heat brought "the supreme test of endurance," Edward wrote, adding that when it was over, "I almost enjoyed the polar breezes while dressing."

The fateful moment when all would look at the Turtles came at daylight. "The House of the Turtles was of heavy logs," Edward continued. "The door was locked and the windows covered. On entering we saw a large table on which was piled a heterogeneous assortment of offerings to the Sacred Turtles. There were fetishes, skins, strips of calico and flannel, pipes, plants, eagle feathers, beads and beadwork, scalps and bead pouches containing umbilical cords.

"The Keeper in a hushed voice rendered a short prayer to the Turtles, begging them not to be offended. He next removed the mass of offerings under which the Turtles were buried so that I had my first glimpse of these mysterious objects. The Turtles were actually turtle drums and beautifully constructed. They were about twenty inches in length and would weigh probably twenty pounds each. The priest explained they were of great weight because each contained the spirit of a buffalo. He kept this belief alive by pretending to exert great strength in moving or lifting them."

The Turtles were decorated with eagle feathers, and Edward took pictures of them in this state. He then asked if the feathers might be removed so he could photograph them without the decorations. "This request occasioned considerable discussion between the Keeper and his helpers," he wrote. "Apparently they figured the Turtles might be offended if left naked by removal of the decorations."

The Keeper prayerfully asked the Turtles' consent to do what Edward asked. With the priest talking to them soothingly, the feathers were reverently removed.

Edward's heart pounded. "At last, after so many months of effort, I was looking at these ancient Sacred Turtles which had been guarded well for so many years from the profane eyes of the White Man," he wrote. "After photographing the naked turtles, I courageously asked the priest if I might move them slightly in order to obtain a better picture. To my surprise he acquiesced, but warned me against turning

The Sacred Turtles—Mandan

them over." If Edward did that, the priest said, all in the room would die.

Holding his breath, Edward gently moved the Turtles on the table to a better light, and photographed them twice more. He backed away and folded his camera. "I am finished," he said.

"I was shaking like a leaf and reeking with perspiration," he wrote. "The fear of interruption before the pictures could be made was a nerve-wracking experience."

As it turned out, there was good reason to be nervous. As Edward and the rest left the House of the Turtles, twenty-five Indians rode up on horseback, suspicious enough, Edward reflected, that they hadn't let the blizzard hold them back. As the new arrivals silently eyed Edward and Upshaw, Edward went through the motions of recording something on an Edison cylinder, trying to look innocent.

"Obviously, they were wondering why I should return in the winter to see the Keeper of the Turtles," he wrote. He struggled not to show haste as he placed his camera and precious negatives in his saddle bags.

"Granted I had paid the exorbitant price of $500 to that avaricious priest. . . . Yet I realized there would be no time for explanations should the tribesmen be convinced of their suspicions," he wrote. "I knew our lives hung in the balance. My muscles seemed frozen when I lifted myself into the saddle. Urging our horses to the greatest speed, we put distance between ourselves and the Mandan."

7. Fifty Men's Work

With winter once again lashing the plains, driving Edward and his crew from the field, he headed back to New York. The first two volumes of *The North American Indian* were about to come off the presses, giving him something tangible to show, and he hoped to line up a good number of subscribers.

There was urgency about it because a financial crisis gripped the nation, to become known to history as the Panic of 1907. The banking system was interrupted more than at any time since the Civil War, meaning that money was not being circulated.

This affected Edward in that the banks which had promised to underwrite the costs of publishing his first two volumes withdrew the promise. The Morgan money, it will be remembered, was to be used only in meeting Edward's field expenses. The panic also meant that fewer people would have money for books.

Edward succeeded in getting several subscriptions which were fully paid in advance. These early subscribers included the British, German, and French ambassadors in Washington, a number of libraries and museums, and of course President Theodore Roosevelt, who wrote in his foreword to the volumes, "Mr. Curtis . . . has been able to do what no other man has ever done. . . . caught glimpses . . . into that strange spiritual and mental life" of the Indians from which "all white men are forever barred."

In mid-December, Edward started back west, stopping off in Chicago where he ran into a new kind of sales resistance to his work. "He expresses skepticism as to any one man doing so much," Edward wrote

For a Winter Campaign—Apsaroke

Hodge about the prospective buyer. "In other words he thinks I have attempted too big a task for one man, saying, 'It looks to me as though you were trying to do fifty men's work.'"

In his home city of Seattle, where people knew Edward Curtis better than the Chicagoan did, he was able to raise $20,000 in loans from friends. For a while at least, Edward's private panic was over. Also, if he had any worries how his work would be received now that it had begun to appear, he could worry less after reading a letter from a man whose opinion carried great weight—Dr. Frederick Ward Putnam, curator of the Peabody Museum of Archaeology and Ethnology at Harvard University.

"It has given me much pleasure to look over the first volume of your great work on the North American Indians," Dr. Putnam began. "Everyone will be pleased with your artistic rendering of the picturesque in Indian life—a phase of the many-sided life of the Indian which has heretofore been neglected from lack of power to present it adequately.

"You belong to the last generation that will be granted the high privilege of studying the Indian in anything like the native state, and all future students and historians will turn to your volumes. . . .

"The gathering and saving of this information is of the utmost importance while it is yet possible, and it is indeed fortunate that this work is to be done by one who has the skill of an expert photographer and the mind and eye of an artist united with a sympathetic understanding of this much-misunderstood people. . . ."

By late spring of 1908, the praise had become a chorus. "Every American who sees the work will be proud that so handsome a piece of book-making has been produced in America," said Dr. Clinton Hart Merriam, who had been one of the scientists Edward met on Mt. Rainier in 1898, "and every intelligent man will rejoice that ethnology and history have been enriched by such faithful and artistic records of the aboriginal inhabitant of our country."

Edward's friend, George Bird Grinnell, who had encouraged him to undertake the project, was especially attracted by *The Vanishing Race*, as many others would be. This picture, Grinnell wrote in *Forest and Stream*, "is full of poetry and pathos, for what could be more significant than the long line of shadow figures passing into the darkening distance."

At the Guildhall Library in London, which had been presented by J. P. Morgan with Set No. 7 of the volumes, librarian E. M. Borrojo was struck by the attention drawn by the books. "Although the Morgan gift has been on view only a day or two in London," he commented,

92

Bull Chief—Apsaroke

"quite a number of distinguished savants have called to inspect it. The librarian has deputized two assistant clerks to show the book to enquirers. . . ."

Financier Henry E. Huntington, founder of the world famous library bearing his name at San Marino, California, and who once paid $50,000 for a Gutenberg Bible, wrote to Edward after he had subscribed to Set No. 51 of *The North American Indian*, "I regard it highly for its effective illustrations and its wealth of information. . . .

Medicine Crow—Apsaroke

I have greatly enjoyed looking the volumes over, and am very glad to
have them on my library shelves."

Charles F. Lummis, librarian of the Los Angeles Public Library and
founder of the Southwest Museum, considered the world's foremost
museum of the American Indian, wrote Edward after subscribing to a
set for the museum, "that no respectable public library can do without
such a historic record. . . ."

Lummis was a kindred spirit, in that he himself had been a photog-

Apsaroke Mother and Child

rapher of the Indians. He had lived with and taken pictures of them for twenty years, in Central and South America as well as in North American. "But," Lummis continued in his letter, "I frankly admit that I have never seen such successful photographs as yours. It simply makes me sorry that I am not able to subscribe to two copies." No subject, he commented, "interests so many people, 6 to 60, as Indians."

"The nature race is melting away," said Professor W. J. McGee, head of the Bureau of Ethnology at the Smithsonian Institution. "Their number, as I estimate it, is reduced to a third or a quarter. They have gone from the forests and plains, from the hills and valleys over which they roamed and reigned for an age, and the survivors are changed. We have taken their land, we have blotted out their homes, their faith, their philosophy; a whole type of humanity. Our conquest has been the most striking in history; near a thousand distinct languages have given way before the conquering Anglo-Saxon speech and the force of the press.

"Lowly as they were, our original landholders deserve a monument; cruel as our conquest was in some respects, it deserves a record; and your great book forms both. I do not know any other general picture of the American Indians so faithful as yours. . . . Indeed, none other is nearly so vivid and accurate."

Indian Commissioner Francis Leupp—no ordinary bureaucrat, but a lawyer, journalist, and student of the Indian since boyhood—wrote, "In other published works, more pretentious than this on their strictly scientific side, are gathered stores of information about our American aborigines. But Mr. Curtis' harvest has passed far beyond the statistical or encyclopedic domain; he has actually reached the heart of the Indian and has been able to look out upon the world through the Indian's own eyes.

"This gives so vivid a color to his writing that his readers not only absorb but actually feel the knowledge he conveys. I do not think I exaggerate the facts in saying that the most truthful conceptions of the Indian race which will ever form themselves in the mind of posterity may be drawn from this great work."

96

Atsina Warriors

Two Leggings—Apsaroke

The New York Times commented, "Mr. Curtis has rare qualities as a photographer, alike in his recognition of the groupings, the light and shade, the points of view that make a picture as pleasing as it is truthful and in his ability to make the picture after he recognizes its value.

"His portraits are better, in the important qualities that go to make good portraits, than are the majority of current oil paintings, while in the other pictures one sees always that elusive quality which can be put into them only by an artist who sees beauty as well as material fact, and when it is all finished it will be a monumental work, marvelous for the unstinted care and labor and pains that have gone into its making, remarkable for the beauty of its final embodiment, and highly important because of its historical and ethnological value."

The volumes reminded the *Literary Digest* of John James Audubon's *Birds of America*, published between 1827 and 1838. "It is not unlike that famous work in the splendor of its manufacture, the authenticity and historical value of its illustrations, or in the methods employed in the collection of the material," the magazine commented.

"A poet as well as an artist," wrote E. P. Powell in *Unity Magazine*. "If it ever comes our turn to vacate the continent may we have as able an interpreter and as kindly and skilled an artist to preserve us for the future."

While these good things were being said about his work, Edward and his crew were pressing forward among the Sioux in North Dakota, bent on meeting Edward's goal of three volumes for 1908. On August 19, Edward wrote Hodge from Minot that it looked as if they were going to succeed—if all kept pushing.

"We sent you the Crow history today and tomorrow will probably send the Sioux history and then will have another bunch of material ready to send in a few days following that," he wrote. "Will get off the final manuscript belonging to these three volumes within a week."

Myers would be leaving for the East in a few days, Edward wrote, "and as soon as he reaches Boston the composition will begin, all of which means rush."

In another month Edward was in New Mexico, writing Hodge from

Santa Fe on September 18 that he had already "closed my short piece of rather trying work here." He continued, "I am happy to say that while I think it has added a few gray hairs it also has given me splendid additional footing in the southern work." What it was that gave him the gray hairs, he characteristically did not say.

Returning home to Seattle, he put in several weeks "hustling things the best I can at this end." Then he was off to New York to see to the publication of the year's quota of work—the completion of Volumes 3, 4, and 5.

"Matters are moving on nicely, and I must express to you my heartfelt thanks for your splendid assistance in keeping everything going," he wrote Hodge on November 11.

As the presses rolled on the three new books, Edward received an offer of help from an English friend who wanted "to do all in his power" to bring *The North American Indian* to the attention of the British public. The Englishman was in a strong position to be helpful. He was Lord Northcliffe—Alfred Charles William Harmsworth—who owned most of London's newspapers and that year, 1908, would also become owner of the *Times* of London, "the Thunderer," as it had been called since the days when poet Thomas Carlyle said of an editor of the paper that he "thundered through it to the shaking of the spheres."

The new volumes came out early in 1909, on schedule, but as Edward traveled west again he was haunted by an old problem— shortage of funds. The Morgan money had fallen far short of meeting his needs in the field. The country still hadn't gotten over the Panic of 1907, and little money was coming in from his books. New subscribers were holding back; the old were slow to pay up.

Edward was so short he couldn't pay Hodge. "I received your letter in regard to funds a few days ago," he wrote his editor on July 13, from Seattle. "I appreciate more than I can tell your great patience in the matter and will say, in the beginning, that I had expected to have been able to pay you all the money due you long before this, but collections have been heartbreakingly slow.

100

A Taos Maid

"Of fifty thousand dollars that should have been paid in during June, I received less than twenty thousand, and just at the present time I am walking the floor trying to keep the banks from growing peevish. . . ."

At the end of another strenuous summer in the field, Edward once more made the long journey across the country to New York, an idea in mind to improve his finances. The idea worked. In a jubilant letter to Hodge on December 10, he wrote, "A couple of days ago I had a final favorable decision from Mr. Morgan in regard to furnishing further capital in the Indian work. It will be settled up now and the money made available as soon as papers, etc., can be drawn up.

"I feel particularly well pleased with this for several reasons,"

Tấpâ ("*Antelope Water*")
—*Taos*

Edward went on. "The added capital will be a tremendous help, and the fact that Mr. Morgan does this proves that he is satisfied with the work so far done and believes in its value. . . .

"Our cause is gaining strength. . . ."

Two days before New Year's, Edward sent Hodge a check for $2,037, making it a happy ending to a hard year for both men. "I hope that it will do its part on a satisfactory start for the New Year," Edward wrote warmly.

For Hodge, too, the new year meant the start of a new responsibility for him; he had been made head of the Bureau of Ethnology.

The year 1910 was only three weeks old when Edward was back in the Far West, spirits high, clearing the decks for another driving summer in the field. "This is my second day of active work in the

102

cabin," he wrote Hodge from Kitsap County, Washington. "We are now getting organized and should be able to make things hum from now on. You probably will hear from us from time to time, as numerous questions will probably come up. . . .

"I wish I could steal you from your office for two weeks and keep you here in the cabin. We are entirely shut off from the world, and our weather is anything but winter from your point of view. Our camp spot is certainly as cheerful as one could wish in this weather, which is the sort well adapted to ducks."

A couple of days afterward, a note from Myers, in longhand on notebook paper with ring holes, hinted at the nature of the work underway as the rain drummed on the roof. "Dear Mr. Hodge," Myers began respectfully, "If Wissler [Professor Clark Wissler, Yale University] has published anything on the Blackfeet later than his preliminary sketch and his Mythology (both of which we have) will you secure a copy and send to us? Sincerely, W. E. Myers."

The work in the cabin was still in progress when Myers dispatched yet another query to Hodge, on March 10, again showing how careful they were to be accurate. "Will you write to Chamberlain and find out what he thinks about the word *Kutenai*?" Myers wrote. "He gives it as a term applied by the tribe to itself. But the Kutenai at Flathead Lake, Montana, insist that the word is used only by other Indians, not Kutenai, and that their proper name is *Ksanka*.

"If the Tunaha were Salishan, as their language indicates they were, then what looked to me as a pretty certain origin for Kutenai becomes questionable, provided Chamberlain is right in saying it is a Kutenai word," Myers went on.

"I sometime ago wrote Chamberlain submitting a number of Kutenai words with probable, or improbable perhaps, derivations, and asked for his opinion, but have heard nothing in reply. Is he inclined to be chary with his knowledge? I should like to hear what he has to say, and if in your letter about the above matter you can incorporate a suggestion that will bring an answer, I shall be grateful to you."

By mid-June, they had finished their task in the cabin and were ready to take to the field again. "We have worked along the Columbia

Kutenai Duck Hunter

Edward Curtis in a Kutenai canoe

River and Willapa harbor and Quiniault," Edward wrote to Hodge on June 18—like Myers, using notebook paper, "and now we will start for Vancouver Island, to be gone some two months. Preliminary information available does not seem particularly illuminating. I take it our hind-sight will be more valuable than our foreknowledge in this case."

Myers had made a scouting trip to Victoria, the island capital, but had come back empty-handed. "Those about that town seem wholly lacking in knowledge or information bearing on the island," Edward wrote, with a trace of impatience. "They tell us that it is a bad season of the year owing to the Indians all being absent. I trust we will find a little material here and there, and at least have an outline of the subject by our return.

"Myers will go east at once on the close of our Vancouver Island expedition and will be ready to take up the book making, so do your best on manuscripts. We should be ready to begin reading proofs in early September."

106

8. Don't Let a Whirlpool Get Us

"As we moved downstream," Edward wrote, "Myers and I made notes, watched for places to land and checked on old village sites. Schwinke set his typewriter on a packing case and hammered away typing yesterday's notes. Some days swift water and rapids kept us busy just staying right side up. At night we camped on the shore. Sometimes we picked up an old Indian and took him along for a few days."

They were on the Columbia River, going to Vancouver somewhat indirectly by first following the historic route of Lewis and Clark in 1805. In those young days of the nation, little was known of the country west of the Mississippi, and Meriwether Lewis, President Thomas Jefferson's private secretary, along with William Clark, brother of the Revolutionary War hero, George Rogers Clark, were on an expedition to find out more.

Starting at the mouth of the Missouri River near St. Louis in the spring of 1804, Lewis and Clark wanted to discover a land route to the Pacific, learn about the Indians along the way, and acquaint themselves with the topography and resources of the upper Missouri country.

They spent the winter among the Mandans in Dakota Territory and in the spring went on to the three forks of the Missouri, in southeastern Idaho, naming the forks Jefferson, Madison, and Gallatin, the last after Albert Gallatin, Secretary of the Treasury. They followed the Jefferson fork as far as they were able, then, with the help of Sacajawea, or

107

Flathead Camp on Jocko River

Bird Woman, they procured horses and crossed the Rocky Mountains.

At a tributary of the Columbia, they built canoes and in these braved the tumultuous river with its racing current, rapids, and waterfalls all the way to the end—to where the river sent its mighty torrent smashing against the Pacific ocean tide.

"I wanted to see and study the region from the water, as had Lewis and Clark more than a hundred years ago," Edward wrote. "I wanted to camp where they camped and approach the Pacific through the eyes of those intrepid explorers."

The craft Edward picked for the trip was not greatly different from the canoes of Lewis and Clark, so far as being a match for the river was

108

A Flathead Chief

Raven Blanket—
Nez Percé

concerned. It was a small, flat-bottomed affair, square at the stern, pointed at the bow, and driven by a gasoline engine with barely enough power to keep up steerageway, even though the course lay downstream.

Besides Myers, his crew included Edmond Schwinke, a stenographer, Noggie the cook, and an old river pilot who wanted to make the run just once more in his life.

At Celilo Falls, where the river fell thunderously over an 80-foot precipice 150 miles or so from the ocean, a flatcar hauled by a tiny loco-motive was provided to portage the boat to navigable water below. Owing in part to high water from spring freshets, which covered the track extending down into the river for the car to ride on, this opera-tion went poorly.

Because Edward was the best swimmer, he worked in the river, di-recting the proceedings, while the others hauled on the lines to pull the boat onto the flatcar. They couldn't hear him above the roar of the falls, however, and he swam ashore to make himself heard. There he found Noggie sitting on the ground weeping, no longer manning his line.

"What in the world is the matter with you?" Edward demanded.

"You'll be drowned," Noggie sobbed.

Edward ordered him back to work and returned to his station in the river. After he had made another half-dozen visits ashore, the boat was finally hauled aboard the car and the portage completed.

At the point where the river made its final plunge through the Cas-cade Mountains in its descent to the sea, locks got them past the worst part, but beyond the falls came a long stretch of whirling, rain-swollen chaos. As they came out of the locks, they tied up to the side of the concrete spillway to talk to the lock crew.

"Several of them knew the old captain," Edward wrote, "and those who did not, knew of his reputation as the most daring and successful of the old river captains. The lock keeper urged him not to attempt the rapids at this season."

The river was at its highest stage, the lock keeper pointed out, and besides, he said, "The currents have changed since your day."

110

The Fisherman—Wishham

Edward, meanwhile, was tuning the engine. "I almost hoped the captain would take their advice," he wrote, "but the captain's only answer was a few grunts. He looked at me and wanted to know if I had the teakettle boiling. 'If you have,' he said, 'let's be on our way.' "

The boat drifted into the stream and was quickly caught by the current, bobbing and pitching like a cork. The captain grinned with excitement. "Boy, this ain't navigation!" he shouted to Edward, who handled the bowsweep. "This is a boxing match. If the old river gets

111

in one blow we're through. Ride 'em high," he called. "Keep her on the ridges. Don't let a whirlpool get us."

Edward did his best. The boat "bucked like a wild cayuse. She stood on her hind legs. She pitched head first into a yawning pit. She shot sideways with a lurch which almost threw me overboard. We rode a long high crest which seemed like a mountain ridge.

"Whirlpools were to the right of us and while dodging them we barely missed one on the left. As we plunged by it, there was another on the right large enough to swallow three such boats. As we sped by, a tree was caught in the swirl. It stood on end and disappeared."

Then it was all over. They steered for shore to rest. Schwinke said the ride through the wild waters had lasted seven minutes. "As a celebration that night we bought a huge chinook salmon from a fisherman and had a feast," Edward wrote. "It was the fattest, juiciest salmon I've ever tasted. We ate until there was nothing left but the bones."

When they reached the place where the Willamette River emptied into the Columbia, Noggie had had enough. He quietly folded his bedroll and left the boat. The old captain, who had wanted to make the trip down the river once more, had richly realized his wish. While Edward and Myers worked in the vicinity, he went into Portland to visit old friends, and died.

At last reaching the Pacific, and seeing it at the approach as Lewis and Clark had seen it, Edward cut the little boat adrift so that, as he wrote, "it might float out to meet the ocean breakers and be battered to fragments."

To take her place for the ocean-going part of the trip, he bought the *Elsie Allen*. Built by an Indian for salmon-fishing in the strait of Juan de Fuca, she was forty feet long by eleven feet at the beam, and besides an engine to drive her, "carried enough canvas for cruising." For all that, she was modest enough considering the waters she would be matched against. Edward hoped for the best.

First, they visited the tribes on the seaward side of Vancouver Island, all going smoothly as they took pictures and gathered information about these Indians. Then they sailed back through the strait of Juan

112

de Fuca, the long passage that separates Washington from Vancouver Island, rounded the lower end of the island, and entered the labyrinthine waters between Vancouver Island and the British Columbia mainland, setting course northward.

They came to notorious Seymour Narrows, where many a ship and canoe had been smashed on the rock that stood out of the water in midchannel. How many had died here no one knew.

Edward planned to anchor south of the narrows, pick up an Indian pilot, and then wait for slack water before trying to go through. But all at once, as they were considering where to anchor, matters were snatched out of their hands. They were hit from aft by the incoming tide and carried forward as if the *Elsie Allen* were a mere chip on the surface. They reversed the engine—nothing happened. The onrushing sea was in command.

"Whatever might be the perils of navigating the Narrows at the worst state of the tide," Edward wrote. "we were in it and there was no escape."

Inwardly, though, Edward relished what was happening. "In the inner recesses of my mind," he confessed, "I was happy in the thought we had no Indian pilot and that we were to experience the hazardous stretch of the Narrows while the riptide was the greatest. I took the wheel from our native and told him to go below and nurse the engine." The native was their Indian contact man.

With Myers standing trancelike at his side, Edward fought the wheel as the boat was propelled toward the rock. "Once in the whirl I had little control of our course," Edward wrote. "At times we spun like a top. Our bow pointed hither and yon; yet on we rushed. Speeding past the great central rock, the breakers and spray poured back on our deck. We seemed to miss the rock by inches."

Not long afterward, as they continued the voyage northward, with the British Columbia mainland to starboard, Vancouver Island to port, they were treated to a different kind of thrill. It came in the evening as they lay anchored in a narrow, twisting waterway among the mountains.

"Our boat was close to a sheer cliff," Edward wrote. "Our evening meal was finished and we were lounging on the deck viewing the eerie surroundings. The gloomy, forested cliffs towered toward the clouds.

"Looking up the channel where the waterway gave perspective, there was a break in the low-hanging clouds, and the snow-clad peaks glistened in the crimson afterglow of a northern sunset. It seemed as though we were gazing from a bottomless pit into paradise. Enveloping us was silence so deep that it seemed audible."

There came a faint, faraway sound, growing rapidly louder. "First it seemed to resemble the crackle and hum of the northern lights," Edward wrote.

All agreed, as they kept their eyes on the upper reaches of the channel, that it was a speedboat.

Carved Posts at Alert Bay

"Then around the bend, perhaps a half mile away came a huge whale and with such tremendous speed it seemed unbelievable," Edward wrote. "When he was close I recognized him as a sulphur-bottom and at least 90 feet in length. From time to time he playfully hit the surface with his tail. The smash of the blow upon the water in that tunnel-like channel was a hundred-fold greater than the backfiring of an automobile."

The whale vanished around the bend, leaving the watchers spellbound by his performance. "The extraordinary speed and the repeated high jumps were possible only because the whale was traveling with an exceedingly swift current," Edward wrote. "The channel was crooked and the bends very abrupt. How the whale in his mad and apparently exuberant exhibition of speed kept from colliding at the turns was beyond understanding."

Edward's northward journey stopped at Fort Rupert, just below the southern tip of Alaska. "As we dropped anchor in the shoal bay on which is located the Kwakiutl village, we saw below the single line of dwellings comprising the settlement," he wrote. "They were largely rough board structures with their gable ends facing the shore. There were also a few scattered totem poles and carved house posts. Many large and beautifully decorated canoes were drawn up on the beach."

Waiting on the beach to greet Edward and his party was George Hunt, with whom Edward had arranged by mail to serve as his interpreter. "He proved trying yet the most valuable interpreter and informant encountered in our thirty-two years of research," Edward wrote of Hunt. "He was tall, powerful, rawboned, grizzled by the passing of more than sixty years of hard knocks, intrigue, dissipation and the efforts of the 'short life bringers.'"

Hunt was the son of an Indian woman and a Scot who was factor, or manager, of the Hudson's Bay Company's post at Fort Rupert. This was the great fur-trading monopoly set up in 1670 by King Charles II, when he granted a charter to Prince Rupert and seventeen others, incorporating them as the "Governor and Company of Adventurers of England trading into Hudson's Bay," with exclusive rights to trade in the territory watered by streams flowing into Hudson's Bay.

George Hunt at
Fort Rupert

As a boy, Hunt had taught himself to write, beginning by copying the labels on goods at his father's trading post. He had gone on copying the labels even after his father forbade it, emphasizing the point by hitting the boy so hard on the head he may have suffered a brain injury. Hunt had mastered the mysteries of reading and writing so well that he had written a book about the complex mythology of the Kwakiutl Indians.

Edward was deeply impressed by this accomplishment. "Aside from the unparalleled work of Sequoya in inventing the Cherokee alphabet," he wrote, "George's volume of Kwakiutl myths is perhaps the most outstanding achievement of an untutored native."

But George Hunt was not easy to work with. He suffered attacks of intense rage—perhaps an outgrowth of the beating his father gave him in boyhood. Edward had been unprepared for this. "At the beginning of my contact with George," he wrote, "I knew nothing of his extreme irritability, bordering on insanity. I soon learned the signs of approaching brain storms and would at once suggest that we do some fishing or go visit his traps.

"Yet there were times the rages would occur without warning. On one occasion natives came rushing to tell me that George was in one of his rages and would kill me." They urged Edward to hide.

"This I could not do," Edward wrote. "George was my friend. I walked down the beach to meet him. I managed to calm him on that occasion, but realized there would be others. In the study of the Kwakiutl I worked with him for the greater part of four seasons. The results were well worth the patience and tact it required. Without his extraordinary assistance, the material for Volume 10 could never have been collected."

9. Stay Clear of the Whale's Tail

As George Hunt sat on the beach watching, Edward waded in water up to his hips a few yards offshore, probing among the rocks with a pole. Soon he found a telltale burrow. He poked at it and waited. In moments the octopus crawled out from under the boulders.

"Its size gave me a chill," Edward wrote, "but not wanting a native to think I lacked courage, I made the grab."

Alas, he missed. The water was too deep and the octopus too heavy. "Perhaps, too," Edward admitted, "I fumbled the catch. At least the creature was not thrown and I was caught. Some of its tentacles were holding fast to the boulder and the others wrapped around my legs. I was as securely anchored as though the job had been done with strong ropes of rubber. The harder I struggled, the firmer grew its grip."

Thanks to his penchant for doing things the Indians did, Edward was captive of a devilfish in waters where these creatures are the largest in the world—the waters off British Columbia. George Hunt had told of once subduing one that spanned forty feet when its tentacles were spread out.

The Indians told spine-tingling tales of devilfish reaching into their canoes and dragging the occupants into the water, doing it so fast that the victims had no time to fight back. One old Indian told of a devilfish that had snatched a canoe by the gunwales, clamping it firmly between two tentacles, while it wrapped a third around his sister. Only by fast action with an ax was he able to save her.

118

Despite these nightmarish stories about the devilfish, Edward still wanted to capture one, doing it the same way the Indians did it—by brawn and main strength. First, he had to find one. They lived in burrows under big rocks far enough out from shore so that the burrows stayed under water at low tide. The Indians found the burrows by wading out from shore when the tide was low and looking for heaps of seashells, cast off around the burrows by the devilfish as they enjoyed their favorite food of crabs and shellfish.

"The hunter, or fisherman, is equipped with a long, slender wand or pole," Edward wrote. "With the burrow located he prods the cavity under the rock. After annoying the creature he withdraws the stick and waits perfectly still. The devilfish, deciding it is better to be elsewhere, slowly creeps from the hole. First the tips of his tentacles appear. Then

The Wedding Party—Qágyuhl

A Nakoaktok Chief's Daughter

Hǎmasaka in Tlǔ'wǔlǎhǔ Costume with Speaker's Staff— Qǎgyuhl

with extreme caution he moves from beneath the rock. The instant the entire body is free, it is off in high gear. The rapidity with which it attains full speed is amazing.

"The catching native, with cat-like movement, grabs the creature and quickly throws it to the beach. The entire success depends upon the quickness of the movement as the octopus must be picked up and thrown before it has time to use its tentacles."

This Edward had failed to do. Things were rapidly going from bad to worse. "I was wearing hip-length rubber boots and on these it vented its rage, cutting innumerable holes through the rubber," he wrote,

121

adding that the octopus's cutting equipment was "shaped like the beak of a parrot, with a razor-like edge."

And the tide was coming in. "Help!" Edward called as the water rose around him, rippling over his shoulders.

George Hunt, who had been enjoying the fix Edward had got himself into, stopped laughing. "George had not seen the octopus so did not realize the gravity of my plight," Edward wrote. "He became a frightened and efficient Indian. With his hunting knife he dived into the murky water. He failed on first and second attempts, but on the third he succeeded in slashing into the body and the vise-like tentacles began to lose their grip. . . ."

Dragged ashore, the devilfish measured eleven feet. For all its loathsome ferocity, though, it was a minor adversary compared to the whale, which held a place in the lives of the Kwakiutl much as that of the buffalo in the lives of the Plains Indians. The whale was their food supermarket and capturing it, Edward wrote admiringly, was "the most daring and dangerous of all activities of the American Indian. The capture of the whale, the largest living animal, by natives in a frail canoe is a tremendous undertaking."

It followed that before they set out on a whale hunt, the Kwakiutl invoked the help of the spirits. They began the secret rituals or preparation, including self-purification, in October, six months or so before the whaling season opened in May.

"We finally broke through the wall of secrecy and secured not only details of the occult ceremonials attendant to whaling, but what was equally important, the legend accounting for their origin," Edward wrote.

He had heard rumors that the whalers kept a mummy in the bow of the canoe, but it was months before someone let slip that this was true, making it necessary to correct a great mass of field notes. Once this information was out, the rest came more easily. Edward won permission to take part in some of the whaling ceremonies—and to go along on a whale hunt.

But first he would need to provide himself with a number of human

Edward Curtis standing by a baleen whale

skulls and a mummy. With a reluctant Myers at his side, Edward set out one night to meet this requirement, visiting some nearby islands used for burial grounds.

"Our craft that night was a small canvas canoe which was ideal for stealthy maneuvering," Edward wrote. "Landing at one of the islands of the dead, I proceeded to look for a mummy. It was not my plan to disturb well-housed or lately interred bodies, but rather to locate an ancient crypt."

He found many boxes crumbling with age, but they held little of what he wanted. "Skeletons were numerous but mummified bodies were not to be found," he wrote. Moreover, qualified skulls, well-weathered, without hair and detached from the spine, were scarce. He could find only two that were suitable.

The second night he gathered four skulls. The rest of what he needed came to him like manna a few days later, when he was out taking pictures. A thunderstorm broke and as he passed under a big spruce, running for shelter, he was showered with burial boxes from the tree's branches, blown loose by the wind.

"In falling they hit other boxes below, and all broke in the descent so there was a veritable deluge of bones and skulls," he wrote. "Like a boy gathering apples, I quickly picked up the skulls, thus adding five more to my collection."

He still had to find a mummy, and he asked George Hunt for a hand. Hunt talked it over with his wife, the Loon, then said to Edward, "The Loon thinks she knows where you can get a mummy and she will help you. It is on the Island of the Dead of her people some thirty miles from here. We should go while the people are away to the fishing village."

The three arrived at the island after a voyage of some hours. Taking care not to be seen, Edward and the Loon went ashore, leaving her husband to look after the boat. Finding the "grave houses," they set to work. "We pried open a few without finding a satisfactory specimen," Edward wrote. "Then good fortune was ours.

"We found a beautiful mummy of the female species. I was not sure whether it was a relative or an enemy of the Loon's. It was quite

evident she knew the lady well, and henceforth always referred to the mummy by name. Before the removal from the box, she talked to it and explained it was a great honor she was soon to receive."

To prepare the skulls for use, George Hunt strung them on a ring of cedar bark, fashioning a kind of necklace. This was worn in some of the dances, the dancer swaying in such a way as to make them rattle in accompaniment to the song he was singing. Now that he had all the needed accouterments, Edward was freely admitted to perform in the secret rites that preceded the whale hunt, including the so-called "mummy-eating ceremony."

But it all counted for nothing. When they went out to look for whales, the whales had left for other waters.

From their performances in staging the legends of the tribe, Edward saw that the Kwakiutl were natural actors. He decided to make a motion picture, *Land of the Head Hunters*, telling the story of their greatest legendary hero, Motana, using the Indians themselves as the actors. He cast George Hunt's granddaughter as his leading lady, in the role of the Princess.

With Myers and Schwinke helping, Edward began work on the film, showing the Kwakiutl "in their great canoes against the grandeur of tribal country," in 1910—presumably on this visit to British Columbia. He carried on the project piecemeal on later trips during the next two summers.

While he was making the movie, he received an injury that would plague him the rest of his life, although he said nothing about it at the time—or at any time, apparently, until years later when he was an old man. The injury came while he was in a canoe, filming a whale which was struggling to escape capture.

"With Indians to man the canoe, we drew close," Edward wrote. "The creature was immense. Perched as steadily as possible in an Indian canoe in a rough sea, I was getting some incredible footage of this monster.

"I urged the paddlers to move closer. In retrospect I wonder that they obeyed my wish. I wanted a closeup looking into his huge throat.

126

A Fair Breeze

Suddenly I was hurled into the sea and fighting for my life beside that thrashing leviathan. The canoe was smashed to splinters; my camera and priceless film at the bottom of the ocean.

"There flashed through my mind the admonition of an old whaler, 'Stay clear of the whale's tail.' I swam frantically hoping to escape that thrashing tail. It was a miracle no one had been killed and we were doubly fortunate there was another canoe near to rescue us . . . but how I mourned that wonderful film made at such close quarters."

Not until a generation later, in 1948, did Edward mention how he got the injury that he had carried with him through the years. He wrote

127

Nakoaktok Chief and Copper

of it then in a letter to Harriet Leitch of the Seattle Public Library. He wanted to clear up his frequent mention of "my bum leg" in his correspondence with her.

"I acquired that lame leg . . . while making a motion picture of a large whale," he wrote. "He became annoyed and with his tail smashed our whaling boat with a swat of his tail. I came out of the smashing with a broken hip . . . I still limp slightly."

Land of the Head Hunters became more than a movie. A friend who read the script suggested to Edward that he tell the story in book form. Edward did so, and the book of the same title was published in 1915. At about the same time he wrote *Indian Days of the Long Ago,* which sold a million copies the first year. Both books were still paying royalties thirty-five years later.

Kalóqǔtsuis—
Qágyuȟl

10. Regulation Snake in My Mouth

It was a blazing August day at a Hopi village in southern Arizona. The Indians were engaged in the Snake Dance, their annual invocation to the gods for rain. With their nearly naked bodies grotesquely painted, the dancers wound round and around the plaza, singing, shaking rattles, flinging snakes around their necks, placing them between their lips, and tossing them to one another.

The fascinated onlookers never suspected that one of the dancers was a white man. When Edward himself had been a spectator to this ancient ritual for the first time, in 1900, he had realized that in order for him to grasp the true meaning of the dance, he could not simply watch from the sidelines, but would need to take part in it. Each year for many years he had gone back to the Hopi to renew his request with the priest for permission to participate.

According to his recollection of the event later in his life, 1912 was the year success was his. He had been initiated into the Snake Order as a priest, probably the first white man ever to have been accorded that honor, and he became, in effect, an Indian. The triumph went far to offset the disappointments of the year before, when lack of funds had kept him from his researches in the field and a lecture tour to raise money only added to his debts.

For sixteen days, the time the snake ceremony lasts, Edward did exactly as the Indians did, with time out to take pictures and make recordings as the ritual went forward. "Clad in a loin cloth, I entered

130

the kiva with the Chief Priest and followed his orders and directions in every detail," Edward wrote. "I slept beside him. I fasted. . . ."

On the tenth day the hunt for snakes began. "We stripped and smeared our bodies with red paint, which is considered the pollen of

A Snake Priest

snakes. At the same time the chief offered a prayer that the snakes would not harm us."

Each man was provided with a stick to dig the snakes from their holes, an eagle-feather whip, a bag, and a small parcel of food. The priest pointed out that wearing little clothing, exposing their bodies to the burning sun, was in itself a prayer for rain, to cool them off. He reminded all to drink only from living springs.

"Then we climbed the ladder from the kiva and proceeded single file down the trail to the land of the north wind," Edward wrote. "The Hopi understand that on this day no one may go into the valley northward from the village."

At the base of a cliff they stopped to drink at a spring trickling from the rock. They prayed and scattered offerings of cornmeal on the water. Then began the search for snakes. Edward was first to see one. "We surrounded it and threw meal on it," he wrote. As required of the discoverer, Edward stroked the snake with his eagle-feather whip, causing it to straighten out in preparation to escape.

"Then I quickly seized it by the neck," he wrote. "As a novitiate, I think they wanted to make doubly sure of my brotherly love for the snakes, for they indicated I must wrap it about my neck before it was placed in my bag." Edward was able to do this without too many qualms, he explained, because of the ritualistic preparations of many days in the kiva before they set out—by now he believed like the Hopi.

There were lots of snakes to be found—most of them rattlers. Their sacks were soon heavy with snakes. At sundown all returned to the kiva, where they washed their catch and put them into earthen jars, to share quarters with the hunters. From the desert they brought in sand which they spread over the floor so that if a snake crawled out of its jar, it left a trail to tell of its passage.

The snake hunt went on for four days, one day in each primary direction—north, south, east, and west. At noon of the fourth day, "we returned to the kiva for our noon meal and thereafter sang seven songs to the snakes," Edward wrote. "When the singing was finished the snakes seemed to be in a lethargic condition."

Watching the Dancers

Hopi girl

Antelopes and Snakes at Oraibi

A day was then spent in the kiva getting the costumes ready for the dance. On the evening of the fifteenth day the Snake Priest called on the performers to arrange themselves in groups of three, each trio to decide among themselves who was to dance with the snakes, who would be the "hugger," and who the catcher.

Edward noticed that even the Indians didn't seem overly anxious to dance with the snakes, and he was not surprised that to a man they chose him. "Having experienced sweat baths for purification through the years while working with various tribes, I knew only too well that the Indian seemed to particularly enjoy giving the white man the full treatment," he wrote. "From now on until the end of the ceremony we had neither food nor drink."

Next came a snake-washing ritual. Hidden behind a blanket, the chief pounded some roots. When these were pulverized they were placed in boiling water, causing a lather to form, the priests meanwhile gathering up the snakes by the neck, three or four to the hand. When the lather had cooled, the snakes were immersed in it, then laid out on the altar to dry.

There were three reasons for washing the snakes, the priest explained to Edward: "Because the snakes are our children, because we hope to be repaid in the form of rain, and also wish their bodies to be clean when we put them in our mouths."

It was time for the grand climax—the dance itself. "We smeared pink clay over our moccasins and other parts of our costume and corn smut mixed with 'man medicine' (a concoction of root juices and whatnot) over our forearms, calves and the right side of our head," Edward wrote. "We whitened our chin and blackened the rest of our face. Around our waist we placed the customary brightly woven fringed belt and in the rear, we hung a fox skin, which moves in rhythm of the dance."

The snakes were brought to the plaza. The Snake and Antelope fraternities lined up facing each other. While the Antelopes sang and shook their rattles, the Snake men by threes began dancing. Each dancer received a snake, which from time to time he placed around

135

his neck or between his lips. The "hugger" danced close behind with his left arm around the dancer's neck, while with the other he stroked the snake with his eagle-feathered whip.

"I followed the dancers four times around the plaza, and tossed the snakes aside to be picked up by the catcher, then received another snake for the continuation of the dance," Edward wrote. "Dressed in a G-string and snake dance costume and with the regulation snake in my mouth I went through [the ceremony] while spectators witnessed the dance and did not know that a white man was one of the wild dancers."

For four days after the finish of the ceremony, with the snakes returned to the desert as messengers to the gods, the chiefs of the two participating clans, along with Edward, remained in the kiva, continuing their prayers for rain. This was an anxious time for Edward. "If it doesn't rain they believe there has been an error in the performance," he wrote. That error could be that they had allowed him to take part, meaning trouble for those responsible—and for Edward.

So Edward added his own, private prayers to those going on in the kiva. He was grateful when "billowing dark clouds formed over the mountains and the welcome rain began to fall."

11. The Tide Brought the Breakers Closer

"J. PIERPONT MORGAN DEAD IN ROME"
Edward joined the cluster of passersby gathered at the newsstand to read the headlines in *The New York Times*. The date was April 1, 1913. Morgan had died the day before at the Grand Hotel after becoming ill in Egypt while he was on vacation.

Edward bought a copy of the paper. Already there was speculation as to who would succeed to the top of the Morgan financial empire. "Mr. Pierpont Morgan, Jr., is a very able man, who has already carried through some very important business in a successful manner, and in the ordinary course one would expect the succession to come to the popular 'Mr. Jack,'" read a dispatch sent from London by Marconi Transatlantic Wireless Telegraph. "There are, however, half a dozen other partners in Mr. Morgan's American business . . . ," the account continued.

The younger Morgan did in fact move up to his father's place, as history tells, but the son soon curtailed the elder Morgan's operations in the art field. Edward feared that support for his work was at an end.

Recalling the events for Miss Leitch of the Seattle Public Library long afterward, Edward wrote, "I at once began an up-to-date financial report on our situation and an account of the project which I delivered to the auditors of the Morgan Bank.

"Sometime later, I received a call from the bank, saying Mr. Morgan's son would like to see me. The following day I made my call. I was literally numb with apprehension, knowing that practically all of the elder Morgan's explorations in foreign lands had been closed; also I knew that all commitments for purchases of art objects and paintings had been cancelled, and that a great part of his paintings were being sold. Considering all this, I could not see how the North American Indian project could be continued."

Edward's worries were soon laid to rest. "Mr. Morgan's greeting was decidedly cordial," Edward wrote Harriet Leitch, "His handclasp gave me hope. Without preliminaries, he began the discussion of the Indian work, stating, 'I can well understand your anxiety as to what's to be done about The North American Indian,' he said. 'As a family we have discussed the matter thoroughly and have decided to finish the undertaking as Father had in mind. We know that's what Father would want us to do.'"

Morgan then outlined the plan he had in mind. "We would discontinue all sales efforts and devote all energy and money to the completion of the field work and publication," Edward wrote. The sales office on Fifth Avenue was to be closed and all business matters handled by the Morgan Bank.

"I was to plan my field season and text work so that I could spend a few winter weeks in New York each year. I at once mapped out plans for the field work to complete twenty volumes. I wrote Mr. Myers of the plans and locations of our coming season's research. We were to start the season among the Mandans and Arikara on the upper Missouri River."

Edward left for the West as soon as possible, anxious to get started on the season's tasks. "The field party was on the ground a day in advance of my arrival," he continued in his account to Miss Leitch. "I reached the camp in the early night and the first man of the party to greet me was a young chap who knew nothing of the upper Missouri. His first words were, 'Chief, how soon can we get away from this d—— place?'

"The tone of his voice annoyed me. 'What do you mean, get away?' His answer was, 'The mosquitoes are eating us up.' To which I replied, 'To Hell with the mosquitoes, we are here to work and will stay until it's finished. If you can't stand the mosquitoes it won't take you but two days to walk out to the railroad.' That finished his yowling and he was dropped from our party at the end of the season."

By early August the work in this area was completed, and Edward was off with the faithful Myers and Schwinke to British Columbia once again. The material for Volume 10 was now in Hodge's hands for editing. "Let me know when you have the manuscript ready for the publishers," Edward wrote as he was leaving for the north. "I will make the few remaining pictures on this trip and with them developed, will be ready for publication."

While he was away, Edward received the sad news from his studio in Seattle that A. F. Muhr had died unexpectedly. Muhr was the darkroom genius who developed *The Vanishing Race* from the plate that had been thought to be underexposed.

"It came at the end of the day's work at the end of the week," Edward wrote to Hodge on November 24, 1913. "I . . . returned as quickly as possible and for the balance of the year I must remain at the studio and get affairs in such shape that I can be comparatively free from the studio burden."

In March of the new year, there was more misfortune. "A bad fire has occurred at the Seattle studio," Edward fleetingly mentioned in a note which he enclosed with a check for $500 on account to Hodge. How bad the fire was Hodge could only guess.

Whatever the havoc, Edward and his helpers were back in British Columbia as soon as the warmer weather of spring allowed. After a few weeks in the wilderness, Edward seemingly began to worry about Hodge and how he was getting along at his end, off in Washington.

"Myers and I are wondering how you are coming on with work on the manuscript," Edward wrote on June 20, 1914, from Port Hardy, British Columbia. "I hope that you have it practically done. Do let us know. . . . Our activities here are such that they should be classified as labor rather than work, but all goes fairly well."

That same year, Edward was made an honorary member of Phi Beta Kappa at the University of Washington.

Near the end of the summer Edward and Myers decided to visit the Koskimo tribe, at the northern end of Vancouver Island, on the coastal side. To get there, they left their boat, the *Hesperus*, in the shelter of Hardy Bay, on the Inside Passage, rather than risk her to autumn storms in the open sea, and set out across the island on foot.

With the party was George Hunt, whose story of the Koskimo tribe led Edward to make the trip. As the four began the hike—Edward, Myers, Schwinke, and Hunt—each man carried a fifty-pound pack on his back, considered a small load. "We were traveling light with limited food, limited cooking utensils, few blankets and the very necessary camera and film," Edward wrote.

Their loads would weigh enough, they would find.

The Fire-drill—Koskimo

"The trail through the heavy, jungle-like forest was rough and deep with mud. The depressions were water-filled, sometimes to our shoe tops and sometimes to our hips," Edward wrote. "The sky was leaking. It was a characteristic 'she rain' of the North Pacific, occurring during the autumn, winter and spring.

"In that area natives classify their rains by sex. A 'she rain' is gentle, caressing, clinging, persistent, but a 'he rain' is quite the opposite in all ways but that of persistence."

In the "she rain" the four sloshed doggedly on, each mile seemingly longer than the last. "The pack straps chaffed and our feet seemed encased in divers' leaded boots," Edward wrote. "Some days are longer than others and this was one of the longer.

"Stumbling and falling in the murky rain-soaked darkness, we came to a deserted fishing shack at the water's edge. Its flea-infested interior was filthy and foul smelling, but we couldn't be choosy. At least it was a place to lay off our heavy packs and park our weary bodies. At the center of the roof was a hole for the escape of smoke. Below it we built a fire and soon our rain soaked clothing was under full steam."

In the morning the rain was still coming, but there could be no waiting for it to end, at this time of the year. "We found an old dilapidated skiff and with a few hours' work we patched the holes," Edward recounted. "Some of us bailed and some of us rowed. Soon the rain changed sexes. The weather gods pulled the plug and we had 'he rain.' Considering the rain and wind and our leaking skiff we made for shore and shelter, but the only shelter to be found was a large cedar tree with thick low-hanging branches.

"Close around the trunk of this sheltering tree we huddled and for twenty-four hours we continued to huddle. A cataract of water poured off the drooping branches. It could not be said that our roof did not leak; it merely kept us from smothering in the downpour. I feared the water would find its way through the oilskin wrapping of the camera and notebooks.

"All things end in time and again the rain changed sexes." It shifted back to "she rain," and finally it stopped. The government weather

141

station told them later that during each of the twenty-four hours Edward and his companions were under the tree, nearly one inch of rain had fallen. The total was twenty-two inches.

"I have been in desert cloudbursts where the rainfall per minute was greater," Edward wrote, "but that was the wettest twenty-four hours I've ever experienced."

It was a month before they got back to the *Hesperus* on the lee side of the island.

With time running out for this season, Edward chose to do one more thing before going home. This was to get pictures of the Steller's sea lion, the largest of its species in the world, reaching thirteen feet in length and over a ton in weight. Their favorite rookery was Devil Rock, standing out of the sea among the Queen Charlotte Islands, thirty miles off the British Columbia coast.

Edward and his party reached the island after a stormy voyage that took two days, spending the final night at an anchorage fittingly named Grief Bay. Although the sun was still not up when they arrived, the light was already good enough for picture-taking, and Edward shot a number of photographs as they approached.

"The island was blanketed with the great beasts," he wrote. "At the pinnacle sat a gigantic bull who towered above all the others. We dubbed him the Mayor. The approach of our boat started a restless movement of the herd. The bulls bellowed and the cows barked in protest. I quickly made pictures from the boat. By this time the sea lions were stampeding. They poured off the rock in a waterfall of unwieldy beasts."

To make the landing, the visitors transferred from the *Hesperus* to an Indian canoe. With the surf pounding against the shoreline rock in great, smashing rollers, careful timing and agility were called for. First to make the leap was Stanley, George Hunt's son. "At the right instant he sprang," Edward wrote. "Myers followed. On each inshore rush of the sea, I tossed them bundles of blankets, food, water, harpoons and overnight necessities."

Cameras and film, wrapped, padded, and put into watertight bags

142

sealed by clamps, were then sent over on a line tossed ashore by Edward. "While my companions were carrying the equipment well above the breakers," he wrote, "I watched for my opportunity and made my spring to shore from the canoe."

As the canoe returned to the *Hesperus*, Edward made his way to the top of the rock, and there made a terrifying discovery—*Devil Rock was under water at high tide!* Barnacles clinging to the rock and pools ablossom with anemones, among other telltale signs, told the shocking story. "The government chart I had consulted was obviously wrong," Edward wrote. "We were thirty miles off the coast and unable to apprise anyone of our perilous plight."

He heard Myers calling. "Chief, do you realize there is no driftwood on this island?" Myers had made the same sad discovery as Edward. Driftwood would be carried away each time the island was inundated. The two gazed off toward the departing *Hesperus*, already well beyond hailing distance.

The chart had shown Devil Rock to be forty feet above water at high tide. "Not a great margin of safety in a storm," Edward commented, "but safe in favorable weather. That the chart could be forty feet in error had not occurred to me. Unwittingly, I had placed my party in this jeopardy. I could hardly find my voice to answer Myers. The young Indian undoubtedly realized the situation too, yet he made no comment. We went about our work as though we had a lifetime ahead. Perhaps luck would be with us once more and we would survive. Yet I cannot read about a human being sentenced to death without recalling that awful moment."

The sea lions added to the aura of inhospitality that hung over the place. "At close range the bulls were so incredibly large they dwarfed us as though we were pygmies," Edward wrote. "These belligerent behemoths resented sharing their quarters. Their dispositions were ugly and the cows equally ill-tempered. This encounter convinced me that natives traveling in canoes on stormy seas to harpoon such great creatures needed all the help obtainable from the spirits to whom they prayed."

Edward took pictures of the sea lions as they swam about in the surf, noisily working up the courage to come ashore. "The Mayor, bellowing imprecations at us, was the first to arrive," Edward wrote. "Soon losing courage, though, he plunged back into the sea. Again he approached, his harem barking encouragement. All of which afforded an excellent opportunity for making pictures."

The day passed and the tide began to come in. Slowly up the rock crept the water, refilling the pools and driving the three trapped men toward the top of the rock. When the sun flattened out on the horizon in a molten red blob, and then was gone, the world left to them measured about 200 by 100 feet and was growing smaller.

This seemed to be the time the sea lions were waiting for. "The restless animals were bellowing and barking in combined protest," Edward wrote. "Apparently they held a conference and decided upon a mass attack. As though under orders from a commanding general, they literally poured upon the rock from all directions."

Edward and his companions tried to stem the invasion by swatting the animals in the face with a pair of five-gallon gasoline cans, once used as floats for harpoons. The sea lions fell back, then came on again. As darkness settled, man and beast seemed to reach a kind of truce and peace prevailed.

The visitors gathered their equipment at the "Mayor's Suite," a flat area at the highest point of the rock. "Edging it was a ridge, broken in sections like the vertebra of a gigantic prehistoric animal," Edward wrote. "These cracks in the ridge allowed us to make fast our harpoon lines. The cameras were placed in their waterproof sacks, securely lashed to the rocks."

The night was calm and starlit. The sea beyond the breakers, with hardly a breeze stirring, was smooth as enamel. To Edward and his companions, it was hard to believe that this could be their last night alive. Then something further took their minds off what might lie ahead.

"We began to realize," Edward wrote, "that the sea lion had cause for his irritability. Our flesh itched and burned. As the submerged por-

144

tion of the rock grew smaller the lice increased in number. It was now time to adjust life lines. Myers suggested I do the lashing."

When Edward had finished making Myers secure, Myers humorously complained, "Chief, you've got me trussed up so tight I can't scratch." When it came Stanley's turn to be tied up against the waves, he asked doubtfully, as Edward made the lines tight, "It it going to be that bad?"

"Fortunately, this is not the season of the highest tides," Edward answered. "But a storm could pile up breakers over our heads. Hold your breath when the waves roll over you. The high tide shouldn't last more than thirty minutes, and there should be a breathing spell between breakers."

The night tide came in with great speed. The water glowed with phosphorescence and drenched the huddling refugees with salt spray, adding irritation to the work of the lice on their skins.

"Relentlessly the tide brought the breakers closer," Edward wrote. "Swells struck with a shattering blow. Darkness compounded our fears. The first wave to carry us off our perch was a terrific shock, but our lash lines held fast, preventing us from being swept out to sea. The uncertainty of what to expect was unnerving. How long could we survive this beating?"

Finally, Edward sensed that the tide had reached its limit. "Then it was a matter of brutal endurance," he wrote. "In about thirty minutes the breakers no longer hit us. Drenched, bruised and bitten, we struggled to loosen our life-saving lines. The chill air on wet clothing set our teeth to chattering. Exhausted from the beating we had taken, we dug blankets out of our bags to cover our drenched bodies, hopefully to get some sleep before daylight."

Edward was awakened by something puffing and dripping spittle in his face. It was the Mayor, towering over him. Edward drove the intruder off with a blow from one of the gasoline cans. "When next I awakened, it was full daylight," he wrote. "My first thought was of the *Hesperus*. I looked far across the sea in search only to discover the boat was almost beneath us. Soon the canoe approached to take us off."

Those aboard the *Hesperus* greeted them with unusual warmth.

They had been sure there would be no survivors on the island. As they had left their overnight anchorage they had met some Indians in a canoe who wondered where they were going.

"George Hunt explained that his son and some white men had spent the night on Devil Rock and they were going out to pick them up," Edward wrote. "The Indians with one voice insisted there would be no use to go. 'Your son is dead for no one can live all night on that rock. Some of our people have taken refuge there when caught in a storm but they always drowned.'"

George Hunt told Edward, "I knew you were drowned. I tried to tell Schwinke, but my mouth was so dry I could make no words. I saw Schwinke's lips move, but he could not speak. Then you stood up."

The Indians had come close to being right; it had been a freakishly calm night. The very next night, as the *Hesperus* lay at anchor at Grief Bay, to give Edward and his companions time to "dry out, delouse and prepare for our departure for the States," as Edward put it, a great storm broke, delaying them three days. By then they were given up for lost by British Columbia officials—the ship, Edward, his party, and all hands.

"Revenue cutters cruising off shore did not see us," Edward wrote. "Nor did we realize they were looking for the lost *Hesperus*. When we did report to British Columbia officials they were disturbed. Their search for us had caused them trouble and expense. To make certain I would be of no further concern to them a police escort was furnished to make sure I was on a steamer bound for the United States."

At least one newspaper in the Middle West had reported "the tragic loss of the Curtis expedition," illustrating the story with a full page of pictures.

12. This One Makes a Better Picture

Florence came down the steps of the train from Seattle and flung herself into her father's arms. She had come to spend a couple of the summer months with him as he worked among the Indians of northern California.

For several years Edward had been slowed in his work by financial problems and domestic troubles, which, in 1920, exploded in disaster. Clara divorced him, and the court gave her nearly all his possessions, including his negatives, the harvest of his life.

He moved to Los Angeles and opened a new studio, managed by his daughter Beth. To add to his income he worked as a still photographer for motion picture producer Cecil B. De Mille, processing the pictures in his own home. When Florence visited her father for some weeks in 1921, while Beth was away, she lent a hand in this by trimming the edges. One famous film Edward worked on was *The Ten Commandments.*

Although racked by fits of depression, he remained determined to see his magnum opus, *The North American Indian*, through to the finish. In 1922 he presented his subscribers with Volume 12, devoted to the Hopi, his very first subjects, and returned to the field with his camera.

"I completed pictures for two volumes dealing with Northern California and Southern Oregon," he wrote Hodge from the new "Home of the Curtis Indians" in Los Angeles on February 7, 1923—for the first time, apparently, in five years. "The pictures for the Northern volume of the pair will be published as soon as we can clear from the first one. I am in hopes of getting into camp long enough to complete pictures for one or two volumes during the coming summer. . . ."

147

So it was that, with the coming of warm weather, Edward was back in northern California, where Florence joined him, at the little town of Williams. In its own way, this new visit with her father in the field was as memorable as the first, when she was a child of seven.

"For all his brawn and bravery, he was a gentle sensitive man and a wonderful companion," Florence wrote of the occasion. "He had a vast knowledge and kinship with the outdoor world in which he lived so many months every year. He knew the trees, the animals, the birds and flowers. Camping with him was an unforgettable experience."

It impressed Florence also that her father seemed to see this kingdom of nature, where he lived so much of the time, in terms of pictures. One evening she selected a spot to put up the tent for the night, only to be countermanded by her father, who pointed to another site. "This is better," he said.

When the tent was up, Florence asked, "What's the difference between this place and the one I picked?"

"This one, my dear, makes a better picture," her father answered.

Edward worked that summer without the usual photo tent, in which he posed his subjects, adjusting the light by moving a flap in the top. There wasn't much room in the Chevrolet coupe in which he and Florence traveled, and he left the tent behind as an unnecessary frill, to make room for the big tent, cots, food supplies, pots and plates, Coleman stove, cameras, film.

But the absence of the photo tent, Florence noticed, seemed to make little difference to her father. If sometimes he wanted to highlight a face in a particular way, he simply posed the Indian under a tree, in a spot where the sun came peeping through the branches.

"He worked fast," Florence wrote. "He was deft and sure. He knew what he wanted, and he knew when he had it. There was none of the usual fussing. He would make two or three exposures, and it was all over—maybe in ten minutes. And he was at it all day long. If he didn't have sun, he took pictures anyway."

Then came a day, among the Smith River tribe on the northern coast, when Florence was sure there could be no picture-taking. A heavy

Curtis's 6½ x 8½ inch Reversible Premo glass-plate camera

On the Shores of the Pacific—
Tolowa

overcast turned the day into half-night, with mist coming from both sea and sky. "I wondered how father would be able to make pictures that day," Florence wrote. "But he did—it never ceased to amaze me."

Edward visited among the little houses where the Indians lived until he found a teenage girl. He paid her a silver dollar and gave her time to dress in her best finery. Then he took her to a bluff overlooking the ocean and there quickly made two or three exposures, as if the conditions were perfectly normal. More than fifty years later, smiling shyly, the young lady still looks sidelong out over the water as clearly limned as in a picture made only yesterday.

"He was friendly but not the least demonstrative, yet the Indians seemed to sense his sincerity," Florence wrote.

Near Ukiah, they camped near a village populated by Indians of several tribes, who had come to the area to pick beans. There were

Florence at a campsite near Ukiah, California

Indians of all ages, from babies to the very old, speaking a half-dozen languages.

One afternoon as the sun sank after a day of 100-degree heat, an Indian girl ran excitedly into Edward's camp. Her grandmother, who had been picking beans all day in the fierce heat, was sick. Would Edward please come immediately?

"We entered a small lean-to hut with earthen floor on which the elderly woman was stretched," Florence wrote. "She looked acutely ill and instinctively I wanted to urge Dad to go to town for medical help. I almost pulled his sleeve to whisper to him, but restrained myself."

Her father quietly expressed his sympathy and he and Florence left. "As we went out the door," Florence wrote, "the medicine man arrived. I noticed it was Dad's interpreter, dressed in tribal regalia."

But Florence was still worried. "Shouldn't we drive to town for a doctor?" she asked her father as the pair walked back to camp.

"No," he answered. "That is for them to decide."

"That answer was very revealing to me," Florence wrote. "He accepted the Indians and their beliefs. He made no effort to change their ideas or way of life or religion, as so many of our race have attempted."

Next day the granddaughter of the ailing woman came back to Edward's camp, her face wreathed in smiles. Her grandmother was much better, she said. Someone had brought a white doctor for her, the girl said, but he couldn't help. "But our medicine man knew what to do."

Several times during the summer Edward and Florence crossed the coastal mountains, visiting first the Indians on one side, then the other. On one crossing they were forced off the road by another vehicle, missing death by the sheerest chance. The car came to rest against an oak tree, teetering on the edge of a gorge a thousand feet deep.

While the car was being repaired, Edward borrowed a canoe and set out to visit an Indian village on the Klamath River, not accessible by car. He took along two Indians familiar with the river.

For Florence it was high adventure. "We camped that night on a

Florence and two Indian guides on the Klamath River

sandy bank of the turbulent river, the air redolent with mingled fragrance of spruce and laurel, warmed by the summer sun," she wrote. "Dad, of course, was chief cook, and I assisted, but he also found time to make me a bough bed that was the greatest I've ever slept on. I thought I knew all about making a bough bed through my girl scouting, but realized I was a novice. His was a work of art, and so comfortable!"

Edward got some fine pictures at the Indian village and next day headed back to the car. Now the journey lay upstream, and it took the combined efforts of all three men to cordelle the canoe against the current.

Watching her father struggle on the rope, Florence became reflective. "I wondered, as I had before and have many times since, if future generations reading *The North American Indian* would have any comprehension of the work it involved and the dangers encountered."

As the weeks passed, Florence became increasingly impressed by her

152

father's skill in preparing their meals. Over a campfire, or using the little Coleman stove—it didn't matter—he made dishes that would be the envy of the most exacting restaurant chef. Florence remembered the squaw bread he had served in Canyon de Chelly long ago, the roast Indian corn-on-the-cob, the kid chops prepared over the coals of an open fire. He had gone on from being a good campfire cook to gourmet.

"As a Roquefort salad expert he had established his reputation throughout the East as well as the West," Florence wrote. It became a tradition in the Teddy Roosevelt family that when he came to dine, he must make the Roquefort dressing.

"I watched him many times. It had to be just so—a time for the vinegar and a time for the oil. Not that he measured the ingredients, but none of us could equal his."

Often they had salmon for dinner. "He was an expert on cooking salmon. It must be cut horizontally, allowing the skin to keep the juices in. Dad was an expert at making cheese omelet, with bread toasted in the pan to go with it. I learned about poaching pears in syrup, and his applesauce had to be made in a certain way. He was very particular about the way vegetables were cooked, so that none of the flavor was lost."

Her father knew he was good. "If he cooked it and you didn't like it," Florence wrote, "then there was something wrong with you, not the food."

By the spring of 1926, Edward could at last see the end of the long road he had started on more than a quarter-century before. He had only two more volumes to go, one on four tribes in Oklahoma, the other the Indians of the Far North.

Then a new crisis struck: Myers, his right-hand man for twenty years, quit. Now he would need to find someone else to sit by his side and take notes as he talked to the Indians, and to go into the field ahead of him and do the groundwork. He could hardly hope to find a replacement as good as Myers, but from his letter to Edward, there was clearly no chance of getting Myers to change his mind.

"An opportunity has presented itself to make a lot of money in the next two years—a real estate transaction," Myers wrote. "It is one of the kind that rarely occur and I am getting too old to pass it up in hope that another will be at hand when the Indian work is finished. . . ."

Still, Myers was not happy at doing what he felt he must do. "As you probably know," he went on apologetically, "the desire to finish the job is what has kept me at it these last few years on a salary that doesn't amount to much in these times and only a very remarkable chance could have induced me to drop the plowhandle. I am sorry this comes so near the proposed date of going to Oklahoma, but the project is only a few days old and did not come to a head until today."

Myers still wanted to be helpful. "As to the field work for the remaining two volumes," he went on in his letter, "it occurs to me that

A Mono Home

Hodge has been confined to his office for a long time and might welcome the opportunity to get away from it. . . ."

Edward passed along this suggestion to Hodge, who now was a member of the staff of the Museum of the American Indian in New York. "It occurs to me that you might manage a vacation of a month or six weeks," Edward wrote. "Join me in the Oklahoma field. . . . From the point of view of *The North American Indian*, this would be the happiest possible solution of what is a serious problem. . . ."

But Hodge couldn't do it. He agreed that it was bad to lose Myers, but he met the situation philosophically. "The news you give me in regard to Myers is a great disappointment indeed," he wrote. "Of course the reasons which he presents and which to him represent the opportunity of a lifetime, even in California, we must accept as the only balm, yet I am mighty sorry the chance could not have been held off until he had finished the excellent work for the volumes that he had been turning out. . . .

"I wish I could go myself, on your account, but this is out of the question, as I am so overwhelmed here that I scarcely know which way to turn. . . ."

Hodge gave Edward the names of two men whom he thought would not "be averse to making a little extra money during vacation," one a teacher at the University of Washington, the other at the Normal School of Fresno, California. But it wasn't until a month or so later that an answer to the problem was found. Hodge wired Edward the good news on May 19, 1926.

"Mr. S. C. Eastwood of Brandon, Vermont, will accept position to assist you in field and write results. Was graduated University of Pennsylvania nineteen twenty-four and is recommended for ability by Professor Speck and assistants. He took anthropology course and is familiar with your North American Indian series."

Stewart Eastwood stepped into Myers' place, and Edward went forward with his plans for the summer. "We are in from the Oklahoma work and I believe we have the material for a good volume," Edward wrote Hodge on October 8, reporting how things had gone. "Eastwood

155

White deerskin dance costume—Hupa

is here with me and will settle down close by while we are whipping the text in shape. Owing to Eastwood's lack of knowledge and experience, I will take the long end of the work in rewriting the field notes. . . . While I am working . . . Eastwood can type his vocabularies. . . ."

Edward wrote that because of Eastwood's inexperience, he had worked by his side during the summer. "I never realized how much knowledge a veteran worker had in his system. . . . College and study cannot give the knowledge and understanding which comes with long contact with the Indians," he commented. "Eastwood has a good ear for phonetics and was particularly capable in vocabulary work."

In another month Edward cheerily reported to Hodge that he and Eastwood were "working like a pair of beavers with but a single tree to cut," to complete the text for Volume 19. "Eastwood grows stronger in the work. . . . I am now thinking of Volume 20. Here is my suggestion: that we make it the Eskimo and one or two of the tribes of northwestern Alaska, including the natives of Yakutat. . . ."

Edward and Eastwood finished with the material for Volume 19

Assiniboin Mother and Child

Black Belly—Cheyenne

late in the winter and sent it to Hodge for editing. To Edward's surprise and chagrin, Hodge returned it, along with a letter addressed to Eastwood finding fault with his work. Eastwood apparently took offense and threatened to quit—all this just as the time approached to start the new, and final, season's field work, in the Far North. Edward wrote Hodge a scolding letter in reply on May 11, 1927.

"You're a good editor but certainly a bum diplomat," he began. "It may seem necessary to wield a club—even so, one might to advantage . . . pad the club. It has taken a lot of quick figuring and hard talking to keep the boy in line. To have him drop out at this last moment would wreck the ship. The office is expecting us to finish Volume 20 this year and to get a new man at this time would be out of the question."

158

The Old Cheyenne

Hodge's return of the manuscript made it necessary for Edward to make a change in plans. "The manuscript is here," he continued. "We have so little time before starting into the field that we will have to put it aside and take it up on our return. . . . The next time you feel inclined to wield the big stick, better address me. I have to stand it. Eastwood does not. . . .

"I leave here on the 25th. The steamer Victoria sails from Seattle on June 2. We go direct to Nome and take a local boat from there to Kotzebue. Our central address for the first half of the summer will be Nome."

Hodge replied promptly, with some more words of his own. "Yours of the 11th is at hand," he began coolly. "Don't take my criticisms, either of you, in any but the way in which I intended it. It is too late

159

to do any jawing after the book is published, so if anybody has a word of complaint, let it be given now, while there is time. If Eastwood will glance over some of my marginal notes, and observe besides that not an Indian term in the whole manuscript is accented to indicate stress, he cannot fail to see two things: that there is a lack of that extreme care which characterizes the other volumes, and that the method of arrangement and treatment has not been followed as strictly as it should have been.

"If I could think that Eastwood has done his level best, there would be no kick coming from me; but I do not believe he has done so, and that's the basis of my complaint. If he will buckle down and take my criticisms as intended solely for the purpose of paving the way to the production of the most faultless book practicable, I know he will see the point and act accordingly. In criticizing a manuscript one cannot help criticizing the author, and I would have done exactly the same thing, no matter who prepared it.

"There is no point of being thin-skinned in a work of this kind. The manuscript is either right or wrong, and if wrong it should be righted. I have enough confidence in Eastwood to know that he can make a very good job of it. If I didn't think so, I would have given up hope, kept the manuscript, and have done what I could with it.

"Of course, I wrote to Eastwood directly, because he sent me the manuscript with a letter. I shall bear in mind what you say about retaining the manuscript until your return from Alaska. . . ."

Hodge ended his letter tersely. "I hope you will both have a successful and enjoyable trip."

160

13. Ice Thick, Fog Closed Down

"The final volume of *The North American Indian* is to be devoted to the Eskimo of the North Pacific and my plans are to devote the full summer season to the work with the Northern natives."

With this preamble Edward began "A Rambling Log of the Field Season of the Summer of 1927," the first account he had ever kept of his work. In deciding to write down what happened as he went at this final stage, perhaps he was influenced by Beth, who was with him for the first half of his northern trip and made daily entries in a "diary letter to the studio."

Edward's own story of his summer in the Far North would fascinate him when he came across it in his attic as an octogenarian. "How I managed to keep that log during all the stress is beyond my present understanding," he wrote to Harriet Leitch of the Seattle library, "yet on reading it twenty years after it was written, it brought the day by day incidents, locations and storm conditions vividly to mind. Frankly its reading gave me the shivers and I constantly marveled that at any time in my life I had the strength and endurance to do such a season's work."

When he had visited Alaska with the Harriman Expedition in 1899, Edward remembered that he had made full use of the fact that, as Harriman put it, "the days were long on both ends." This time, twenty-eight years later, he planned to extend not only the days but the season at both ends as well.

"Will leave Seattle for the North on the first steamer for Nome and come South on the last one sailing from there," he wrote. "To cover the necessary ground and secure the material needed is the logical work of at least three seasons but I feel we must try to do the work in one year. Good fortune being with us we may, by working under great pressure, manage to finish the task in one season. . . . Let us hope for the best and do our best."

Pushing through ice fields most of the way, the *Victoria* took twelve days to get to Nome, robbing Edward of precious days at the beginning of the season. He began at once to look for a boat, either to buy or to charter. Local mail boats were few and most didn't go where he wanted to go. He soon found that no owner would charter him a boat for the kind of trip he had in mind. "They know the uncertainty of the Bering Sea and the Arctic Ocean," he wrote in his log.

Nor were there many to buy. "We have looked the water front over and find but one boat which will answer and possibly can be had," Edward noted. "The owner will tell us tomorrow whether he will sell or not. So much for our first day in Nome."

To Edward's great relief next day, the boat owner, known as Harry the Fish, said yes—with conditions. "It took much talking . . . and he is already sorry," Edward wrote. "The boat, while not much of a craft, is the pride of his heart and to get him to sell, we agree to sell it back to him at the end of the season and take him with us to run the engine."

The *Jewel Guard* was forty feet long, twelve feet wide, and drew three-and-a-half feet of water. "It was an ideal craft for muskrat hunting in the swamps but certainly never designed for storms in the Arctic Ocean," Edward recalled to Miss Leitch.

At seven-thirty in the morning of June 28, Edward set sail for Nunivak Island, 300 miles south of Nome, in the Bering Sea. "Our party aboard," he wrote, "is Beth, Eastwood, and Harry the Fish, and myself. . . . All going well we should make it in three days. We are navigating by dead reckoning (and have no log line—there was no log line to be had at Nome). Dead reckoning navigation without a log line is just a matter of looking at the compass and using your intelligence and trusting to God."

Beth and Edward Curtis aboard the S.S. Victoria

At midnight, after battling ice and strong winds all day, Edward entered in his log, "Ice thick, headway slow, fog closed down so cannot see two boat lengths. Danger of collision with ice. . . . Decide to lay to and drift with ice until better visibility. Harry and Eastwood turned in for two hours sleep. I remain on watch. Gloomy night, wind howls thru rigging and there is the constant sound of grinding, shifting ice.

"At times the little craft is in a spot of open water, again completely packed about by ice. Not so good a start. From the wind and movement of the ice I know it is a bad storm but being in the ice pack there is no sea. This is the darkest hour of the night. I can when on deck see to read. This is a cloudy somewhat foggy night and while it is not dark there is a gray gloomy light and distant visibility is poor."

Seven days later, four days past the time Edward estimated it would take to get to Nunivak, they were still at sea and Edward wrote, as another night began, "The sea was wild and growing worse. It was a sparing [*sic*] match with one big swell after the other. With full power we could make a mile an hour and each breaker looked as though it might be our finish."

In the early morning they took refuge behind a sandspit and decided to lie "at anchor for a few hours and let the storm blow itself out." Venturing back into the open sea, Edward soon saw that the risk of trying to go on was too great. He looked for a chance to bring the boat about and head back to the shelter of the sandspit.

"As she climbed a big swell, I eased her off slightly and as she came to the crest, threw her hard over," he wrote. "Being flat-bottomed, she spun on the crest of the swell like a tin pan and in a flash we were about and running before the wind like a scared Jackrabbit."

But it was no use. Near midnight, blinded by a dense fog, they struck a sand shoal, the engine dying at the same moment. "The instant we hit bottom the sea broke over us until it was all one could do to keep from being washed overboard," Edward wrote. "Each swell carried us a little further onto the sand flat."

At the same time the tide was falling, and presently the *Jewel Guard* was "solidly aground, parked on the floor of the Bering Sea," fifteen to twenty miles from shore. As they sat there in the small hours, the storm howling about them, Edward worried about ending up on some unwanted beach as castaways.

"The condition of my lame hip is causing me a lot of anxiety as

164

I can only go as far as we can get in a boat," he noted in his log. "I could not walk a mile if all our lives depended on it."

Near dawn the tide came and went, but moved the boat only 100 feet. "Fifty feet more and we would have been free," Edward wrote. At noon the tide came and went again, and still they were "sitting high and dry on the sand flat, which extends as far as we can see."

Finally, at six o'clock, the *Jewel Guard* floated and they moved to safety, anchoring in the lee of the shoal that had hung them up. "Oh, boy!" Edward wrote joyously, "What a relief it was to feel her floating free! . . . All hands are smiling. . . . We had a celebration supper of eider duck with dumplings, and tapioca pudding with apples."

Early next afternoon, moving out as the storm eased slightly, they were soon hard aground once again, 100 yards from their old position.

Edward Curtis photographing the Jewel Guard *aground in the Bering Sea*

Uyowŭtcha—Nunivak

Boys in Kaiak—Nunivak

The evening tide, however, lifted them free, and after an hour's battle to work the boat out of the shoal breakers, they were at last on course to Nunivak. They arrived there on July 10, twelve days after they had started from Nome.

The first thing was to find Paul Ivanoff, who was to serve as interpreter during the visit. The natives raised a flag to signal him and moments later he came aboard, "bringing a happy smile with him," Edward wrote, adding, "We are going to like Paul. Paul is part native and part Ivanoff. He is here on the island in charge of the reindeer herd for the Lohman Reindeer Corporation. He had been here for four years: has a small store, it being the only one on the island."

Edward fell to work at once, he and Eastwood spending the entire day ashore. "The natives here are perhaps the most primitive on the North American Continent," Edward wrote. "We should get some good material. We know now our decision to visit this island regardless of the problems, was a wise one. Think of it. At last, and for the first time in all my thirty years work with the natives, I have found a place where no missionary has worked.

"I hesitate to mention it for fear that some over-zealous sky pilot will feel called upon to 'labor' these unspoiled people. They are so happy and contented as they are that it would be a crime to bring up-setting discord to them. Should any misguided missionary start for this island, I trust the sea will do its duty. . . ."

All went well even as the weather changed on the second day at Nunivak and it rained. "Work ashore in Paul's cabin," Edward wrote. "We are certainly fortunate here. Paul is a good interpreter and is good enough to drop all his work and help us. He is about King of the Island, has the confidence of the natives and can get almost anyone to talk with us. Worked on text until noon, the afternoon being sunny I made pictures."

One day Paul had his reindeer herd driven in so that Edward could take pictures of it. "Paul is proud of his herd, insists it is the best in Alaska," Edward wrote.

The same day, they beached the *Jewel Guard* and repaired the leaks

167

Beth Curtis

caused by the pounding she had received on the sandbar during the storm. The following day, July 16, Edward took pictures. Eastwood gathered text material, and Harry the Fish stocked the boat with fresh water.

While they were at Nunivak, the power schooner *Shumanagan*, bound for Point Barrow, the farthest north point in Alaska, put into the island, not knowing at first where she was. The schooner had been on course thirty miles west of Nunivak, but had been blown astray by the storm. Edward learned from the schooner's captain that another boat had been driven ashore at St. Lawrence Island, victim of the same weather.

"Well," Edward observed with satisfaction, "we do not seem to be the only ones who had a hard time during the storm." He went on

168

humorously, "The Shumanagan got 80 miles off course in 250 and had they been where they thought they were, they would have been 400 miles from where they were—if that is not Dutch for you I do not know what is."

Shortly before leaving Nunivak, Edward agreed to give transportation to three other visitors to the island who wanted to go to Cape Etolin, at the north of the island. Two of the men were collecting for the National Museum and the third was a bird collector. Edward was not pleased either with the men themselves or with what they were doing.

"It took two hours to get all their equipment and plunder aboard," he noted scornfully in his log. "They are like a bunch of infants and should be home in the hands of a wet nurse. Why are such inefficient men sent out? While their work is presumably supported by the Bureau of Ethnology, the U.S. National Museum, the American Association for the Advancement of Science, and the American Council of Learned Societies, they are working on limited funds and their getting about must depend on charity transportation of school boat, revenue cutter, trader, school teacher, etc. Hoboing in the name of science.

"At Nunivak they used nickels for money. The natives here did not know one coin from another. Great was their disgust when they reached Paul's store with their nickels. A nickel in Alaska is about on a par with a German mark anywhere. Their plunder consists largely of skulls and bones, about a ton of said human bones in sacks. A skull or two as types might be all right but what in hell do they want with tons of the stuff?

"Harry just about went on the war path when he found that we had a cargo of bones. He insisted that 'Now we will have hell.' I tried to encourage him by explaining that we were only moving the stuff thirty miles. His answer was, 'It doesn't take thirty miles of sea to wreck a boat.' Too well I know that. . . ."

Edward delivered the trio to where they wanted to go, but not without adventure. Sailing at six o'clock in the evening, they were soon in the grip of a new storm, fighting wind, fog, and mountainous waves.

169

"Our passengers lost no time in getting sick," Edward wrote with further disapproval.

The worst part came when they reached the entrance to the harbor at Cape Etolin, at about two o'clock in the morning. In the stormy blackness of the night, the trick was to find the opening.

"Paul was at the wheel and held as close to the shore breakers as he dared, watching and listening for the entrance," Edward wrote. "I think he depended more on sound than sight. The sea was growing wild as we came to what Paul thought was the channel. We swung in. If we hit the channel we were safe. If we missed it we were saying 'Good morning' to St. Peter.

"We hit bottom, bumped over that, then hit again; then we were in the channel and shot through the surf into calmer water. It was a trying five minutes with everything at stake. Harry took a second to howl in my ear, 'I told you the damn bones would be our finish!' "

But the fury they escaped was mild compared to what came thirty minutes after they were inside and safely anchored. "A howling gale from the northeast, not a baby storm this time but a real one," Edward wrote. "Looking out to sea: the breakers at the shoals are rolling mountain high. . . . Wind increasing. It is certainly a wild night. What luck to be in this safe harbor."

For three days they were bottled up by the storm, unable even to land the three passengers, for whose convenience Edward had got himself into this situation. Then, in the small hours of July 26, the storm slacked off. Everyone was up at three o'clock, preparing to leave, but it was five before the *Jewel Guard* got underway.

"It took us a couple of hours to get the bone hunters and all their plunder ashore," Edward wrote, with a final note of distaste.

With friendly weather, it took only an hour and a half to get back to where they had started four days before, in contrast to more than eight hours to cover the same distance on the outbound voyage. Now it was time to leave Nunivak.

"Closed up all matters with Paul and then took him aboard for a farewell lunch," Edward wrote. "Paul has been one of the best helpers

Woman and Child—Nunivak

A Man from Nunivak

I ever had. It was hard to say goodbye to him. In fact, we all left Nunivak and our friends there with a real heartache. I suspect that much of our liking for the island is our deep regard for Paul and through his help our work on the island has been a great success."

When they arrived back in Nome, after pausing to visit the Hooper Bay natives, whom Edward called "the filthiest human beings on the globe," and being storm-bound three days at Golovin Bay on Norton Sound, Beth left for home. She departed by airplane, a highly unusual way to travel in 1927, becoming the first woman to fly between Nome and Fairbanks. Her pilot was Joe Crosson, the famous bush pilot.

"Beth has gone and we will certainly miss her," Edward entered in his log. "One thing is certain, she has not had a dull time while with us and aside from the thrills, she has seen a lot of the country."

It had not been easy for Beth to leave her father. In her own log she wrote, "I was so fearful I would never see him again."

There was good reason for her concern.

172

14. It Is Finished

Beth knew that as her father moved farther north with the waning summer, the weather at the same time would grow steadily worse. Where he was going, navigation ended and boats were pulled out of the water by the end of August—less than a month from now. In addition, there was the matter of his ailing hip.

Edward was not unconcerned about this himself, though it is doubtful if he mentioned it to Beth—or anyone else. At nine-thirty in the morning of August 7, as they set sail for King Island in almost the exact middle of the Bering Strait, he confided to his log, "My hip is giving me much trouble today. The work of getting outfitted and loaded kept me on my feet too much.

"One might wonder how a person can manage this sort of trip with a bad leg. The how of it is that I sit down while at the wheel, that is, when it is not too stormy, and do all the cooking sitting down.

"From my stool I can reach the stove, the dish and food locker and the table. I often prepare a meal, serve it, and do up the dishes without getting to my feet. It is surprising how much one can do sitting down. Naturally there is much of the work aboard which necessarily keeps me on my feet but I save myself all I can. My fear from the start has been that I might become completely disabled but I am keeping up well and I do not think my hip is much worse than when I started. Last year's work in Oklahoma was a hard one on my hip. I suspect it is fortunate that this is the last volume as I have a feeling that this thing may be permanent. Let us hope not."

At midmorning, Edward noted that they had met the schooner

Trader, her deck crowded with passengers, coming from the Diomede Islands, at the upper end of the Bering Strait. "The Trader is the first boat of any kind that we have met since we started on the cruise," Edward wrote. "This is a striking illustration of how little traffic there is in this Bering Sea and Arctic Ocean Country. One swimming about here waiting for a passing craft to pick him up would have a long wait."

All went well at King Island, a sheer rock pinnacle standing out of the sea, where they arrived at midnight. This was "the darkest and worst hour," Edward wrote, but the weather was remarkably calm, allowing them to anchor and land at the one tiny spot on the whole island where this could be done. For a few minutes it looked as if they might be devoured by dogs. There were "countless numbers of them, all one type, large wolf-like beasts," Edward wrote.

"As we anchored the pack set up such a howl that we feared landing might be a problem, but as our boat reached shore we found that there was no ground for fear. Rather than being cross, they were so glad to see a human that they almost crushed us with their affection. They gathered about us so thick that it was difficult to walk. Every dog in the pack tried to get close enough to touch us. Half a dozen at a time would jump up and try to get their paws on our shoulders, and countless dog fights resulted from this rivalry to be our pals."

King Island lies directly on the route of the walrus herd on its seasonal migrations to and from the Arctic Ocean, and Edward wanted pictures of the cliffside huts on stilts where the islanders stayed while they were there each spring and autumn to hunt walrus. The rest of the time they lived in Nome.

"At our visit," Edward wrote, "there was not a human on the island. We expect—at least hope—to get back to Nome before the people have returned to the island, and get our text material from some of the old men there."

By noon the mission had been accomplished. "We are through at King Island and almost exploding with joy at our success in getting our pictures of the village," Edward wrote happily.

174

The Jewel Guard *anchored at King Island*

Pulling up anchor, they sailed north to Cape Prince of Wales, jutting into the Bering Strait from the Seward Peninsula, at the narrowest point between Alaska and Siberia, and the farthest west point of the North American continent. They reached Wales by late afternoon.

"We caught a fair wind and a fair tidal current, and for us made great speed," Edward wrote. "We are certainly in good luck so far on this leg of the cruise. The day is perfect and no sea to speak of. Matters are going so well that I am suspicious of what may come next. Such weather is not right but the barometer is still up."

They quickly picked up the interpreter they were to meet at Cape Prince of Wales and headed for Little Diomede, in the middle of the Bering Strait. They could see the island as they set out, then a thick fog settled down ominously.

"Not so good," Edward noted in the log. He remembered what his friend Rank, the "Daredevil Trader of the Arctic," had told him in

175

Nome. Rank had once spent two weeks looking for Little Diomede without finding it. "He told me that if one wanted trouble all he had to do was to fool with the Diomedes," Edward wrote. "The location being in the Bering Strait, where meet the blows of the Bering Sea and the Arctic Ocean, there is a chance of no end of trouble."

But their luck still held. The fog cleared and they anchored at Diomede well before midnight. Edward cooked breakfast at three in the morning, and by four-thirty everybody but Harry was ashore. "We lost no time getting to work, Eastwood gathering text material, I making pictures," he wrote.

One of the first pictures he took was of Big Diomede, lying a few miles farther west, in Russian waters. "I quickly changed to a long focus lens and with my tripod standing on American soil, I photographed sections of Siberia," Edward wrote.

All day the calm, sunny weather continued to belie the fearsome reputation of the Diomede Islands among mariners as "the storm center of the universe." This was where, it was told on the island, that a boat with school supplies was three years getting the supplies off-loaded. "The wife of the missionary tells us it is the only perfect day this year," Edward wrote. "In fact, the best day she has seen in the four years she has been on the island."

They completed their work at Little Diomede within the day and moved on to Big Diomede, three miles from Siberia. Then the smiling weather ended, with an onslaught of wind, rain, fog, and thundering seas.

With the wind screaming from the northeast, they doggedly worked ashore all day, but after supper they reluctantly changed anchorage to get behind a reef.

"Fog so thick that we hated to move for fear we would lose sight of land, in which case we would have difficulty finding the island again," Edward wrote. "Lost an anchor in moving and came near losing our island. A trying hour."

Two days later, with the *Jewel Guard* swinging by her anchor chain to within a hundred feet of destruction on the rocks and with the seas

176

as high as the mast, they received signals from the natives to shift anchorage to the lee of the southern point of the island, a mile and a half away.

"Shifting was no small or easy task," Edward wrote. "The boat was rolling so that one could hardly stand, and the wind so strong that to breath one had to turn his back to it."

It was good that they moved because, for several more days the storm kept topping itself as if to make up for the deceitful behavior of the weather when they first arrived at the Diomedes. As the tumultuous hours passed, Edward found time for frequent entries in his log. "We need Beth here to cheer us up, but I am certainly glad she is not with us," he wrote after sixty hours of the ordeal.

"Still the same old blow," he wrote next morning at four-thirty. "It has been a long night. One cannot sleep even when worn out. The worst of the blow so far was from 11:00 to 3:00. It certainly was bad." He added, as though to reassure himself, "Certainly it must end sometime."

As darkness fell again, with no letup in the storm, he wrote wearily, "The beginning of another long, trying night. My 6 by 8 camera is ashore. If not for that I think we would end the suspense and try for the mainland in the morning, but I must have the camera."

That night was "the worst yet. We have now passed through five days of strain. Cooking is a problem. To eat, the boys sit flat on the floor with a deep dish between their knees. Land is but 300 feet away and no human could reach it. At this point there is nothing but a sheer cliff 800 feet high. One certainly envies the birds."

Then it was all over. When the *Jewel Guard* reappeared out of the fog back at the old anchorage at the village, the natives thought they were seeing a ghost. "They had taken it for granted that we had been wrecked," Edward wrote. "They now call our boat the Ghost Ship."

Edward and his crew put in a final hard day ashore, winding up the work still to be done, and late in the night set sail back across the Bering Strait to Cape Prince of Wales. "Do not want to chance another storm here," Edward noted in his log, keenly aware there was no more time to lose if he hoped to finish his Far North mission before the arctic winter closed in on them. It was already a nip and tuck race against time.

At Cape Prince of Wales they put Arthur, the interpreter, ashore, and pulled out at once for Kotzebue—farther north still, on the Alaskan coast, above the Arctic Circle. They were favored by a south wind, and they must get to Kotzebue before it changed. "We could not make this run in a north wind as the winds here are unbroken from the Arctic," Edward wrote.

The south wind held and as twilight fell, Edward entered in the log, "We are now out of Bering Strait and dealing with the Arctic Ocean. Since noon our course is just about on the Arctic Circle and will be until about 3 A.M. and then we pass to the north of the Circle. I am too fagged for words. A week with no sleep to speak of has about done me out. I turned in this morning as we left Wales, and that was the first sleep for forty-eight hours."

For three weeks they worked among the natives of Kotzebue Sound, taking pictures and learning their history and beliefs. Then there was no more time; any day they could be trapped by the arctic winter. Already there were abundant warning signs.

"Storm all day, snowing hard," Edward wrote in his log on September 8, 1927—long after all other men had gone ashore and gotten their boats out of the water for the winter. "I asked one of the white men here if this was not an unusually early winter. His answer was, 'No, we usually get some bad weather in early September, then it clears up and we have some nice Indian summer. Of course it is rather cold but seldom gets colder than ten below.'"

Edward commented drily in his log that he had no interest in Indian summers at ten below zero.

In two more days they said good-by to their friends and were on their way, setting sail at six-thirty in the morning. They reached the entrance of the sound by the end of the day—and there, at the threshold to the open sea, they were suddenly hit by a fierce head wind, seemingly as if nature were warning them not to venture farther.

Jackson, Interpreter at Kotzebue   *Charlie Wood—Kobuk*

Edward prudently decided to anchor until morning. As the boat lay under the eerie grandeur of the aurora borealis, which flung a shimmering rainbow across the night sky, Edward wrote in his log, "We are hoping that the wind will drop a little during the night. All the land is white now and we realize that winter is nearing and we need to get our boat back to Nome without delay."

The weather did improve during the night, and at two-thirty in the morning they were underway again. "Wind has dropped and it is a beautiful morning," Edward wrote. "Let us hope it will hold for thirty-six hours, which should take us to Wales."

Despite the lateness of the season, Edward planned to stop at Wales "to do a few days work."

But the good weather was short-lived. At midmorning the sea began leaping and the barometer was falling sharply. "The storm is on us," Edward wrote at four-thirty in the afternoon. "Heavy head wind, bitter cold, heavy snow. On the plains this would be termed a blizzard."

In a few more hours he added, "Visibility is ten degrees less than pea soup."

The fury of the storm increased. The gale snatched the boat out of Edward's hands and blew it broadside to the sea, driving it toward the unseen shore. At a time when they should have been nearing Cape Prince of Wales, they were back at their old anchorage at the entrance to Kotzebue Sound—they had gotten nowhere.

And there was chilling new trouble. Edward discovered it when he was awakened by "something about the slosh of the boat in the ground swell" a couple of hours after they dropped anchor.

"As I jumped from my bunk my feet were in water," he wrote. "I quickly ran aft. The engine room was all awash, a foot of water over the floor. Harry and Eastwood were asleep. While they were crawling out I started to pump. It is evident that in the storm we have worked a seam loose and now we have another problem. To find a place where we can beach the boat and make repairs might take a week and if we are to get the boat back to Nome this fall there is no time to lose."

The dilemma presented its own solution before the day was done. "By keeping the pump going one third of the time we can keep the water down, so we have decided to risk the run without making the repairs," Edward wrote. "It is a risky thing to do but I can see no other way out. . . . The finish of our cruise is getting interesting if not a bit sporting."

He could not have guessed how much excitement lay ahead. They reached Cape Prince of Wales safely enough, but a new storm kept them from landing. As the gale rose, causing the anchor to drag and threatening to drive the boat onto the rocks, it was decided to make a run for a small bay that offered more protection, about fifteen miles to the south.

"Harry had the engine going before he was half out of his bunk," Edward wrote." Between snow and wind-driven spray, everything was a smother of white and every second the storm was driving us closer onto the beach. . . .

"My hunch was we had about one chance in a thousand. One nice thing about such situations is that the suspense is short-lived. You either make it or you don't. . . . The human brain is a strange piece of equipment. When one is brought quickly face to face with a trying situation he does, without any feeling of fear, what would at normal times seem impossible."

At the new anchorage, reached in the blackness of four o'clock in the morning, they had breakfast; then Eastwood went up over the mountain to Wales, only four miles away by land, to start the work they were there for. But the storm became steadily more violent, and in place of being able to return to Wales and join Eastwood as the hours passed, Edward had to run to new safety. This time he headed for Port Clarence, sixty miles away, the only real harbor on the Seward Peninsula.

Through it all, Edward kept his sense of humor. "Between keeping the water pumped out of the leaking hull and shoveling snow off the deck, we manage to keep busy," he wrote in his log. "It is not so much a matter of shoveling snow as it is of chopping ice. It is so cold that the spray and seas that slop on deck combine with the snow, forming solid ice. Where we are or what headway we are making no one can tell. The snow is so thick that we cannot see any distance."

After forty-six hours of blind sailing, they groped their way into the entrance of the new sanctuary, barely able to make out the shorelines on each side. As they anchored at the village, Edward was reunited with old friends. "As a member of the Harriman Expedition I was on the sandspit at what is now Teller thirty-one years ago," he recalled nostalgically in his log, referring to the town built on the site in the years since his first visit.

After being gone four days, the *Jewel Guard* was back at Wales to pick up Eastwood, who had begun to accept the prospect of spending the winter there. Edward made pictures until dark, then helped Eastwood close up the text work, the two boarding the *Jewel Guard* at one in the morning.

"Harry was so mad that he was frothing at the mouth," Edward wrote. "Barometer falling rapidly and storm threatens, and he could see no reason why we had not sailed before dark."

Harry was more worried than conditions seemed to justify. "It was a beautiful calm night with a comfortable stern breeze," Edward de-

Start of Whale Hunt, Cape Prince of Wales

scribed it. "To take full advantage of favorable conditions, we hoisted all our canvas."

But by daylight Edward entered in the log that "Harry was right. We didn't choose to get away from Wales soon enough."

The gentle breeze had become a raging gale, and once again the storm was more or less in charge of things. "We lost no time in lowering our sternsail," Edward wrote Miss Leitch in Seattle years later. "By the time that was done it was obvious that an attempt to lower the mainsail would be suicidal. Harry was sticking his head out of the hatch and shouting, 'Didn't I tol' you so! Now we'll all be drowned!'"

The gale increased, driving the boat faster—a laggard being shooed from the sea at a time when she was likely the last craft afloat between there and the North Pole.

"With Eastwood I stood at the steering wheel," Edward wrote. "Fol-

182

lowing breakers submerged us waist high. The speed of our chip-sized craft gave the feeling that we were a duck being blown from the top of one wave to another. The motor was largely racing in the air. . . . Eastwood in his customary casual way remarked, 'Chief, while I still have a chance, I want to tell you that my season with you has been the big event of my life. Good and bad, I have enjoyed every hour of it.' "

They shook hands.

An hour later they rounded a sheltering cape and were out of the wind. "Seemingly every inhabitant of the village was at the landing to greet us," Edward noted. "My friend Jackson [banker Grant Jackson] said, 'The last wireless from the North said you were last seen starting for the Diomedes and were no doubt wrecked in our first big winter blizzard.' "

So ended the final trip for *The North American Indian*.

Back in southern California, Edward and Eastwood took up the waiting manuscript for Volume 19, returned by Hodge for more work just before they left for the North; and in 1930, the long road that had begun thirty years before came to the end, with the publication of Volume 20.

Looking back along the way at those who had stood by him, Edward wrote in his final introduction, "Great is the satisfaction the writer enjoys when he can at last say to all those whose faith has been unbounded, 'It is finished.' "

Left: Beth, Katherine, Edward, Florence, Harold, and Edward Curtis Graybill (foreground) in Medford, Oregon, 1929

Below: Edward Curtis on his eighty-third birthday

Afterword

Edward Curtis apparently never grew old save in body, keeping active and making plans to the end. Some years after his magnum opus about the Indians was done, he was in the Mother Lode country of California, excitedly preparing to make a fortune by reclaiming zircon from the tailings left behind by the gold miners a century before. "He'd lost all interest in photography and zircon was the only thing he thought about," his friend Angus McMillan remembered. When nothing came of the zircon venture, he lived for a time on a small farm east of Los Angeles, where he raised chickens and ducks and grew vegetables and avocados.

Even after Beth and her husband, Manford E. Magnuson, took him into their home on West Fifth Street in Los Angeles, Curtis looked to the future. In 1949, at the age of eighty-one, he was deep in researching and writing the story of gold. *The Lure of Gold*, he called his projected book, getting behind in his autobiographical letters to Harriet Leitch. "For the last few weeks I have devoted all my time to Spanish America and that's a *big* field," he wrote her July 11, 1949. "The territory to be covered is 5000 by 5000 miles square, and the names of the men involved in the Conquest would fill a book. To date my notes on Cortez fill six sheets of this size. . . ."

By November he was "so busy with the lure of gold that everything else is neglected," he wrote Miss Leitch. "Two walls of my room are covered with pads of research notes. . . . Since I last wrote you I have added several hundred books to my collection. All of them must be indexed and the source given. . . . In the research I have written words enough to fill a half dozen books. . . ."

In the spring of 1950, going beyond library research, Curtis had plans to go to Brazil to investigate some matters firsthand, but something had gone wrong. "An ocean-going ship had been purchased, refitted and put in condition for a trip up the Amazon," he wrote Miss Leitch on May 11. "We were to set sail from Long Beach, California, follow the Pacific shores to the Panama Canal, pass through said canal then south on the Atlantic's shores to the mouth of the Amazon, then a thousand miles up the Amazon to the Rio Negro River. . . ." But "friction and jealousy" had split the promoters of the venture, and it looked as if it would never get underway. "No words can express my disappointment," Curtis wrote. "During all my active life time I have wanted to see the Amazon and the Andes Mountains." Curtis hoped something might still be worked out, then added in seeming abashment at having shown the depth of his feelings, "Arthritis seems to have gone to my head as well as my hands."

In the autumn of 1951, progressive infirmity still had not broken Curtis's spirit, apparent as he explained in a letter to Miss Leitch on August 4 why it had been so long since he wrote her last. "The reason . . . is that my right hand is so crippled with arthritis that I can scarcely hold a pen or pencil. Another reason is that I am nearly blind and that no improvement is possible. Despite this gloomy verdict I have taken great care of my eyes and I can see fairly well."

Edward S. Curtis died of a heart attack on October 19, 1952, at the home of his daughter, Beth, in Los Angeles. Fame had been fleeting. Although many papers throughout the country carried the news, *The New York Times*, in its obituary, gave Curtis two short paragraphs—seventy-six words all told. The paper identified him as an "authority on the history of the North American Indian." In its final sentence it said, "Mr. Curtis was also widely known as a photographer."

Index

Page numbers in **boldface** refer to photographs.

189

VICTOR BOESEN, a former newspaper reporter, war correspondent in World War II, and magazine writer, is the author of several successful books, including *Doing Something About the Weather*, named by the National Science Teachers Association and the Children's Book Council as one of the outstanding science books for children for 1975. The book was also a Junior Literary Guild Selection.

Mr. Boesen lives in California, where his research for this biography naturally led him to Florence Curtis Graybill, who had also been collecting material for a book about her father. Their collaboration has resulted in an adult pictorial book on the same subject.

FLORENCE CURTIS GRAYBILL, herself a journalist, spent two memorable summer seasons in the field with her father, Edward Curtis—one as a child and another when she was older. Years later, while living in Los Angeles, she spent many hours with him, writing down his experiences working with the Indians, and when he became bored, they frequently roamed to the Museum of Natural History. He was, in her words, "the best guide one could possibly have."

Mrs. Graybill provided material for the documentary film, *The Shadow Catcher*, and is coauthor of two books about Curtis. She lives in southern California where she gives lectures and continues to write.